To Antonio
Good luck with
all that you're
doing to have a
positive impact on
Autism generation
5/9/13
[illegible]

Unlikely Saviors
The Book
&
Philanthropic Project

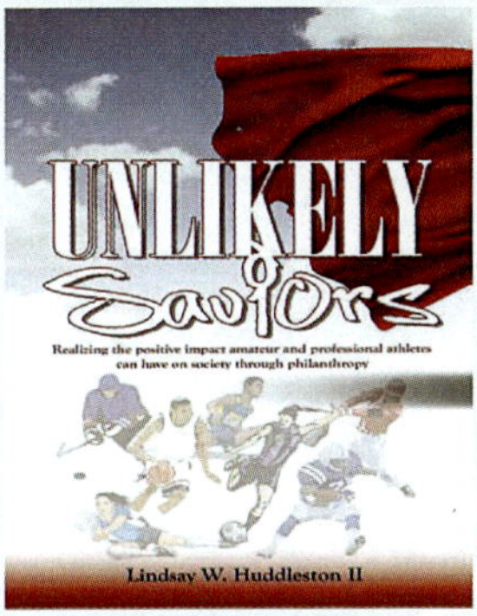

Unlikely Saviors: Realizing the Positive Impact Athletes Can Have on Society Through Philanthropy

Philanthropy is Love

Unlikely Saviors

A service-learning business with philanthropic results.

youtube.com/unlikelysaviorsbook

/unlikelysaviors @unlikelysavior

Unlikely Saviors
Philanthropic Project

Based on sponsor support, the Unlikely Savior Philanthropic Project is a free program to middle, high school and college student-athletes and students-leaders that promotes the merits of community service and philanthropy through hands on student created projects.

Book Contributor Horatio Williams at his Horatio Williams Foundation Team Shoe Giveaway

Telling students during the USPP how they can use their popularity to promote philanthropy

"By involving youth in philanthropic deeds, research has shown that as adults, these individuals will continue to give and/or serve the sector in a variety of ways" (Agard 2002).

Corporate Sponsorship Benefits:

Increase brand loyalty
Create awareness and visibility
Reinforce your image
Drive retail traffic
Drive sales
Showcase community responsibility
Showcase products
Merchandising opportunities
Differentiate products from competitors
Recruit future employees
Combat larger ads and budgets of competitors
Achieve multiple objectives at one time

Foundation Partnership Benefits:

Become a sponsor/mentor for student projects
Help judge student philanthropy
New membership recruitment
Help develop future leaders
Develop future board members
Create sustainability for organization
Build succession plan

Discussing the meaning of "philanthropy" with students during the USPP Presentation

Showing students how to give a firm handshake following the USPP Presentation

Lindsay Huddleston Biography

Metro Detroit Book Signing

"Two thumbs up!" Student approval for the USPP Presentation

Signing books for students following the USPP Presentation

Lindsay Huddleston is a nati Detroiter and former high school teacher and basketba coach. He has traveled the United States and Canada a motivaitonal speaker. Presently, along with being t Founder and CEO of The Huddleston Consulting Grou LLC, a motivational speakin non-profit and political consulting company, Lindsay has been a lobbyist for a Fortune 1 Corporation in whi he managed several million dollars in charitable giving to communities throughout America.
For more information visit:
youtube.com/huddlestong

Lindsay's message of promoting philanthropy to the next generation is resonating throughout the United States and abroad. Lindsay is also, available for book signings.

For books, USPP Presentation (school year and sum camps) scheduling and payment options or to become a USPP Presenter
Contact: Lindsay Huddleston
(313) 414-7378 LH@unlikelysaviors.com
www.unlikelysaviors.com
YouTube Broadcast Yourself™ **youtube.com/unlikelysaviorsbook**

Unlikely Saviors

Realizing how amateur and professional athletes can impact society through philanthropy

Lindsay W. Huddleston II

The Huddleston Group Consulting, LLC
Lansing, Michigan

ISBN: 978-1-4675-0126-2

The Huddleston Consulting Group, LLC is a motivational speaking, nonprofit, government relations and political campaign consulting firm. Our motto is "We Meet Your Needs With Integrity."

Library of Congress Cataloging-in-Publication Data

Huddleston, Lindsay W.
Unlikely saviors : realizing how amateur and professional athletes can impact society through philanthropy / Lindsay W. Huddleston.
p. cm.
ISBN 978-1-4675-0126-2
1. Athletes--United States--Conduct of life. 2. Athletes--Charitable contributions--United States. 3. Sports--Social aspects. I. Title.
GV706.8.H84 2011
306.4'830973--dc23

2011050753

Printed in the United States of America

This book is dedicated to our first child, who will be entering the world this year, and the amazing women in my life, including my loving and supportive wife, Rachel; my strong and intelligent mother, Patricia Jackson; and my wise and caring grandmother, the late Madeline Bryant.

BOOK COVER LOGO EXPLANATION

The Unlikely Savior is represented by a phoenix in the middle, which was known for being a mythical and sacred bird. When the phoenix's life was nearing an end, it would set itself on fire and allow itself to be consumed by the flames. Then there would be a rebirth of the phoenix and it would arise from the ashes in the midst of the flames—renewed.

On either side of the phoenix are two griffins. Griffins are thought to be an especially powerful and majestic creature. The griffin was also considered king of the creatures, their appearance symbolizing intelligence and strength. Griffins are known for guarding treasure, priceless possessions, and the divine.

Above the phoenix is a crown that is the headgear for royalty. The space in between represents the growth that needs to take place in order to be fit to wear it.

Philanthropy is Love is the motto we must remember. God is love so being philanthropic is doing God's work.

Unlikely Saviors is the name of the book that represents those people whom society would not expect to save future generations.

Table of Contents

INTRODUCTION

Swagger—
To move with confidence, arrogance, sophistication, and to be cool. To conduct yourself in a way that would automatically earn respect.

While attending the 2011 Michigan High School Athletic Association Boys Basketball State Championships, I decided I needed to write this book. It was there at the Breslin Center in East Lansing that "swagger" was on full display. These young men displayed a level of confidence and in some cases "star power" that could not go unnoticed. Also, their fellow students and even adults showered affection and praise to these student-athletes comparable to what college and professional athletes receive. The conversations going on around me (even after changing seats between games) were all about why certain athletes were the best players on the court, where they were going to college, and personal facts about the student-athletes' families and lives. The amount of personal attention and public scrutiny given to these student-athletes is more appropriate for professional competitors. With this attention and scrutiny, it's easy to see why so many of the student-athletes develop a sense of personal awareness that can develop into this confidence or arrogance that defines the term swagger.

The key point here is that the student-athletes' popularity gives them a platform amongst their peers and adults. In so many cases, it's the latter part of the "swagger" definition—the arrogance—that gets the student-athletes into trouble. Because they are knowledgeable of the fact that they are held in such high regard, these students take advantage of that admiration, make bad decisions and end up falling victim to their own fame. The theme in the many interviews I conducted is that we must make these student-athletes fully aware of the power and influence they have and guide them to use the platform that society is giving them to use their powers to benefit others instead of only themselves.

There are too many athletes and sports-based charitable foundations to mention in my first book; I anticipate future volumes to highlight many others. Because I am a native Detroiter and former high school junior varsity basketball coach still residing in Michigan, "I'm starting where I'm at" in regard to my research on this topic of sports and philanthropy. That's why my book will have a strong Detroit sports theme. However the message of the need for amateur and professional athletes to use sports as a positive platform is the same despite geography or socioeconomic status.

1

Murder to Excellence

"314 soldiers died in Iraq/509 died in Chicago."
—Kanye West, *Murder to Excellence*

Amateur and professional athletes come from all over. Those who are from America's inner cities—Detroit, Chicago, D.C., L.A., New York, etc.—have a unique potential to address the social ills that plague communities like theirs throughout the country.

This chapter opens with a disturbing comparison that a controversial entertainer states on his new album *Watch the Throne*. West declares, "There is a war going on out there we ain't safe from." Our American streets have always been a hotbed of unnecessary violence (one can argue if any violence is necessary but that's another discussion), however in 2011 we have seen unprecedented spikes in violence throughout the country. This has included cities like Philadelphia, Chicago and my hometown of Detroit. Forty people were shot in two days in Chicago during what is now being called "50 Hours of Violence." In Detroit, a 24-hour span saw nine people wounded and six others killed by gun violence in the city.

I reference the violence in these cities because these are the communities that house many of the future generation's leaders. I firmly believe that by exposing these young people to principles of philanthropy they will become empowered in a way to positively impact the roots of the negative issues that plague their communities. And who better to address these issues than those who are at ground zero and know the mindset and motivation of the one who would pull the trigger? Did the shooter believe that the victim disrespected him? Was the shooter trying to gain a reputation as a "gangsta"? Whatever the reason, these young unrealized role models can most identify with the rationale and more importantly pose the potential to positively address these issues in the most creative manner.

The promotion of mentoring, education or creative arts-based programs can have a significant effect on the behavior of young people. Unfortunately, other methods of intervention have failed and failed miserably. So why not use a new platform, based on the celebrity of amateur and professional sports, to gain the attention of this next generation and help provide a platform to expose young people to the world of philanthropy and giving back? Unfortunately, the millennial generation overall is not familiar with "giving back." As a whole, they are inexperienced with doing something "for free." It's important that they be broken of that selfish mindset now, so future generations will not suffer because of a break in the chain of generations of philanthropic giving. Young people, no matter what their backgrounds, need to be made aware that community service and philanthropy should be a part of their lifestyle and not just a holiday activity.

However, while researching this book I realized that before I can adequately expose, educate, and inspire young people to become philanthropists, they needed to have a sound financial management background. This came to me after attending a workshop put on by The Reach Out Project based in Detroit.

This nonprofit was started by my very close friend Eboni Jones. I actually call her my big sister because she graduated from my high school a few years before me and called me her little brother then. The beauty of Eboni's spirit shines through the moment you meet her. Several months ago, after landing in Detroit from a trip to Dallas, I got an e-mail from her needing assistance with the startup of her nonprofit. At the time, my e-mail signature read, "The Huddleston Group LLC provides consulting to nonprofit organizations." When she read that on my e-mail, she said she believed me to be a Godsend because she wanted help bringing her nonprofit vision to fruition.

Little did Eboni know, she was well on her way to success. My meeting with her only confirmed that she had the right plan in place. I encouraged her to have a launch event and she put together an amazing banquet that honored young people and addressed some pressing social issues like teen abuse. Following the launch, The Reach Out Project had weekly meetings that allowed teenagers to come and express themselves and discuss the challenging issues that impact them and their future. When

I attended, there was a Financial Literacy forum taking place and that's when it hit me. How could I expect some young people who had little financial literacy to be able to embrace the concept of philanthropy, which is giving away money and time? I knew right then that unless I addressed the issue of financial literacy, I would be doing a disservice to the purpose of this book and the future generation I wanted to impact.

This revelation of a need to address financial literacy led to another eureka moment. How can young people put financial literacy in place if they don't have the basic skill set to get a job, to get the money, to eventually give it away? Needless to say, that called for a few extra words to be written. So I decided to continue to keep the theme of my book about athletes and philanthropy, but add 10 pointers on the subject of philanthropy, financial literacy, and workforce development. I chose workforce development because my past role on the Corporate Affairs team for the largest retailer in the world—Walmart—exposed me to the challenges that many employers, both small and large, face. Even when they want to hire hundreds or even thousands from the communities they serve, there is not a surplus of able-bodied, job-ready applicants to choose from.

This idea is not solely focused on urban America. Workforce development and financial literacy are issues that affect suburban and rural America as well. The star power of athletes can be used to bring attention and resources to address these issues. Young people just need the right introduction. This is the reason why I have created the Unlikely Savior Philanthropic Project. The Unlikely Savior Philanthropic Project is a free program to high school and college students and student-athletes that promotes the merits of workforce development and financial literacy along with community service and philanthropy through hands-on, student-created projects. In response to educators pushing for more online options, the Internet, Social Media and this book, *Unlikely Saviors*, will be the key resources used.

To view photos of the individuals interviewed in *Unlikely Saviors* and learn more about our programs, please visit www.unlikelysaviors.com.

2

Coming Where I'm From

"Fronting in the hood trying to be somebody"
—Anthony Hamilton, *Coming Where I'm From*

My story started like so many others. I grew up the youngest of two boys to a single mother in Detroit during the early 1990s. My parents divorced when I was born (I always joke that it wasn't my fault), and my mother, Patricia Anne Jackson, raised Sean Lindsay Huddleston and Lindsay William Huddleston II on Detroit's west side near 7 Mile and Evergreen Road. My mother had some great backup in my grandmother, Madeline Bryant. Like so many young people, we did not quite know our socioeconomic status. Although we felt we had just about everything we needed, we were actually right on the cusp of being middle class. The "Big Three"—Ford, Chrysler and General Motors—employed many Detroiters. My mother, whose education concluded a year short of graduating from the University of Michigan-

Dearborn, was always in finance. Throughout my childhood and young adult life she was employed at the wonderful gem, the Detroit Institute of Arts (where I am a proud former member of the Founders Junior Council and past co-chair of the iconic Fashbash). Currently she is a Financial Analyst for a Chapter 13 Bankruptcy Trustee. In reflection, I think that along with her committed parenting, her jobs also provided me a certain level of worldly exposure that impacted my confidence and approach to the world.

This certainty is evident in my high school and college experiences. As a freshman at Detroit Henry Ford, with some prodding by one of my favorite teachers, Mrs. Melanie Nunn, I was encouraged to run for freshman Homecoming King. As Mrs. Nunn explained, "someone from my class always wins." This was a huge leap of faith for me as a freshman, but I won! No one else ran against me but that's beside the point. Unbeknownst to me, I had a platform that eventually allowed me to have a positive influence on students from my freshman to senior year.

My older brother was a popular senior and all of my "other big brothers" who were friends from up the block were very positive and popular individuals. They encouraged me to have fun, crack jokes, talk to girls and be nice to their parents. Although small, I was a forced to be reckoned with early on.

Enter my love of sports—basketball in particular. As a little league baseball player for the Detroit West 7 league, I would use the excuse of my coach being a few minutes late to pick me up for baseball practice as a reason to go play basketball instead. I LOVED basketball (and minus the surgery for a broken bone in my hand and ACL surgery I still love it, but choose golf over hoops). At any rate, after making the varsity basketball team as a sophomore, the demands on my time were too overwhelming. I went to Coach Weatherspoon and told him I had to step down. He suggested I go to junior varsity. It was a great decision because it allowed me to continue to flourish as a player but more importantly it provided more time to pursue my other passion—politics.

By the time I was a senior in high school, I had to have the same conversation with my new coach, Bill Carter. I left the varsity basketball team my senior season. My rationale was I could either be the last man off the bench for basketball or be the star player in politics. I chose the latter and by the time I graduated from high school I was president of my senior class, president of the student council, president of the Detroit City-Wide Student Council and Youth Governor of the State of Michigan. Needless to say those experiences gave me amazing and invaluable insight that still benefits me to this day.

Upon graduating and after a little politicking, I was accepted into the famed Morehouse College. The great Dr. Martin Luther King, Jr. attended this internationally known Historically Black College. As great as this news was, my family's financial reality became evident when I had to leave Morehouse after my freshman year because as a single parent, my mother could not afford the then $20,000 annual out-of-state tuition. I transferred to Western Michigan University (thanks to the wise recommendation of my life-skills teacher, the late Shirley Jennifer, who encouraged me to have a backup school). While at Western I eventually befriended the late president Dr. Diether

Haenicke. Our relationship began when I was vice president of the school's NAACP chapter, and threatened to protest if the school did not honor Dr. Martin Luther King, Jr.'s birthday with a day off from classes. I am very proud to say that following my negotiations with Dr. Haenicke and president of the NAACP Steven Banks (who still remains one of my closest friends), classes were cancelled and we held a march in Dr. King's honor. We made history. Presently, classes are still cancelled and the march still takes place in honor of Dr. King.

Dr. Haenicke later became instrumental in assisting me with an internship in Washington D.C. with Congressman John Conyers. I also interned with Detroit Mayor Dennis Archer, who remains a mentor to me. After attaining my degree in Political Science, I returned to my alma mater, Henry Ford High School, and replaced my former teacher as an English teacher and basketball coach. I also spent time coordinating the GED and life-skills program at the Benjamin Carson Academy located inside the Wayne County Detention Facility.

I then moved on to travel the United States and Canada as a motivational speaker. I've spoken to several thousand young people about the importance of making high school and college count. Following that experience I worked on Jennifer Granholm's campaign for Governor of Michigan. She won and I later became her Lead Advance, then Law Clerk, and eventually Deputy Director of Legislative Affairs. This was my final role with the Governor's administration before transitioning into the private sector at Walmart, Inc. as Senior Manager for Public Affairs and Government Relations. While at Walmart—a Fortune 1 Corporation—I managed several million dollars in charitable giving to communities throughout America. I also established a track record of unprecedented legislative and public relations accomplishments in Michigan and throughout other parts of the country. Presently, I am the Founder and C.E.O. of The Huddleston Consulting Group LLC, which is a motivational speaking, nonprofit and government relations consulting company. My company does business throughout the United States.

Not bad for a kid who grew up in a single-parent household in Detroit. I credit God, my strong mother and grandmother, and a host of positive male figures in my life, including Earnest McCoy and my late great Uncle Joseph Brooks.

In my past role as a manager of millions of charitable dollars, I learned the great value that philanthropy has. However, I also recognized that there is a huge disconnect between where these dollars originate, whom they impact, and how they are impacted. This is part of the reason I was moved to step out on faith with The Huddleston Consulting Group, LLC.

3

EGO

"I am the GREATEST!" —Muhammad Ali

Dr. Alan Goldberg wrote that before he actually was the greatest fighter ever, Muhammad Ali proclaimed to anyone and everyone who would listen, "I am the GREATEST!" His brash and cocky manner made him simultaneously beloved and hated by all those who knew him. Ali's "I am the GREATEST" attitude highlights one of the most significant parts of sports: The athlete's EGO.

While working on this book at TOAST, one of my favorite restaurants, I had an interesting conversation with Nicole Higgins, a Wayne State University Psychology major. I minored in Sociology in college so I had a basic understanding of the Id, Ego and Superego. We had a great discussion regarding the impact of ego in sports.

Our conversation started with me telling Nicole about my book project and my plans to focus on ego. She asked if I was trying to centralize the discussion on ego.

Nicole explained:

You're trying to centralize it where it's more explainable in detail and that's a difficult thing to do when you're talking about psychology. When you talk about psychology it's just a long-standing theory, it's not rooted in fact. That's the hard part about psychology. Again I think you may want to gear your research temporarily toward the Super Ego to start because that tends to focus more toward the superficial. By text description or interpretation, the Super Ego deals with internalization of what may be considered social norms (mostly in regard to admiration, yes people, mothers). Once those things are internalized the receiver can view them as either right or wrong; but to you or me, it is the opposite. For example, some of the negative behavior athletes display may be wrong to us, but from their perspective, it is not wrong because they have internalized it as being all right. The id on the other hand deals with reality and what the truth is about situations. Remember that psychology is heavily based on various theories so interpretation and perspectives will vary as well.

This is a theory, not fact. Basic Freudian psychology states that you have the Id, Ego and Superego. I think the part you're leaning toward is the Superego. This is just my opinion. Once the athletes transition to becoming superstars, what do you do with that superego? Because they are no longer aware of whom they are, whom have they become when the fans go away, the cheering stops and the flashes no longer exist. I think athletes have that problem.

If you're wondering if the Superego stage is who they really are, it's almost as if they have to answer that themselves. Is that who you want to be? Let's use Michael Vick as an example. What if Id for Michael Vick is the person who is caring and loves dogs? Then we have the Superego. We have the athlete, we have the money, and dogs were killed. The media vilified him. Is that who he is?

Then we have the Id, which is who he self-identifies with in the first stage. This isn't based on age, rather life stages. Who you were at 16 is not who you are now. It's wherever it happens. From that moment in time when you were the Id, are you that person now?

If you believe that the Superegos of the student-athletes still need to be fed after they are no longer playing, and this can be accomplished through philanthropic work, that's a valid theory, but it's a decision they have to make for themselves. The bottom line stops with them.

At each stage there is a choice. That's not something that's in the text, but something that you get to examine after talking and analyzing. It's something that someone may come to, some people may not. It's a choice.

These kids may also have other social factors that play a role. For instance, the example of the student-athlete who feels pressure to leave college early for the pros in order to take care of his family. You ask how this player can come out of that Superego when he has all the social factors pressuring him to succeed, which is a good question. If you take away the fame and the attention that they have received and have become addicted to, how can you break them out of that?

It's valid that you compare that situation with an athlete raised in a caring, loving home front with a message of, "No matter what you do, you are a success and I will still love you the same."

Jimmy King

"I'm more than just a basketball player."
—Jimmy King

I had an opportunity to sit down with Jimmy King, one of the members of the University of Michigan's Fab Five and arguably college basketball's top recruiting class member. King was recently hired to run and facilitate sports programs for H.Y.P.E. (Helping Youth Progress & Excel) Athletics, a Dearborn-based nonprofit formed in 2001 to help communities organize diverse athletic events that are free from drugs and violence. We discussed the concept of Ego, beginning with what made the Fab Five so unique.

Jimmy explained:

> Initially what made the Fab Five unique is that we were already socially conscious before the fame. We had to attribute a lot of that early on to our parents and our upbringing and teachers and schooling and coaching. We knew that we had responsibility to others and not just ourselves but to our families and to our communities to be more than just basketball players and athletes. So early on I can attribute our awareness to our upbringing and to our parents. We were physical examples first by the way we came together, played together, and interacted. Then when people started

paying attention we got a little bit more notoriety and it grew from there. But at first it had to do with our families, upbringing, and surroundings.

Often we get pigeonholed into just being athletes. Coming up, people know just one thing, which is the sport that we're playing. It's almost a shock to people that we can do something else. I don't think people realize how short an athletic career can be, even if you're blessed to have such a career. They can last anywhere between five and 10 years with 10 being a very good career. Anything over 10 is great. At that point, depending upon when you came out of school—whether you stayed one or two years or came straight from high school—and if that's so, then you retired at the age of 30 to 32, maybe 34, 35 years old. You have another 60 years of your life and what are you going to do with that? You have to be more than a basketball player. The truth is that you have to spend more time being more than what people know you for. You have to prepare for that.

I'm not knocking coaching because I'm a coach myself; I'm not knocking athletics but we have to learn more in the realm than just being the best player. You want to be the best citizen, the best community leader, the best person, the best father, the best son, and you can learn all that through athletics early on. The discipline that's taught in sports is one of the same basic principles that translate to being successful in business, successful in the community, and successful in life. But you have to learn more than just being the best player. We have to understand that growing up.

Now that I'm out of the game and coaching, I instill that in my kids and to the people that I touch. When I go speak at camps I tell them that realistically, they can reach their goal and shouldn't let anyone tell them they can't. But they also need to understand that they are going to spend most of their time being something else other than a professional athlete, if they're even blessed enough to do that.

I think we drop the ball when we tell our kids to focus on being professional athletes. I say we should point them in the direction of being professional businessmen, or businesswomen, or doctors or lawyers. Focus on something that's going to sustain you for 50 years instead of 10. The reality is that yes, of course we love to play the game; if we are fortunate enough to take it to another level and make a living out of it, then that's a rare blessing. So I give the kids the percentage of what it takes to become an athlete. There is only a very small percentage that become football or basketball players. That's a low number when you compare the odds of becoming a doctor, lawyer, or even mayor. I tell the kids to think of it like this. If you have a goal to play in the NBA, there are only 400 jobs in the world for you. As you get older and closer to your goal, that path narrows. Give yourself a chance to have something to fall back on. You have to have a Plan B because life is going to deal you different cards that you may not be prepared for. But you will be prepared for them as long as you get your education toward whatever respective career you enter. Do not be pigeonholed as an athlete and think that you can only make it through football, basketball, baseball, or whatever your sport may be.

It's not to say you want to crush their dreams to be professional athletes. But we have a responsibility to tell them the truth. I'm not going to sugarcoat it and say my career was all great and we all can do it. No, that's not the reality. There might be one professional athlete in the whole group I'm speaking with and oftentimes I'm already it. However, it's also important that with this reality, we encourage them to do their best and not let anyone—me included—tell them what they can't do.

It's as though we're all standing in a burning building and there are two exits. One you have to actually climb a 20-foot ladder to get out of small window or you can run out of a wide open door that allows 20 to 30 people to get out at one time. Which door are you going out of?

Another important concept to share with amateur athletes is the psychological aspect of sports and that's ego. The ego is so powerful for kids during their amateur years and even into pro careers, but can be dangerous if an athlete believes so much of that while trying to transition into life after an athletic career.

It's tricky because you have to have an ego to be

good. People are going to tell you how good you are coming up and you're going to start discovering that you can separate yourself in your sport and you will start to develop more of an ego. I'm not saying an ego typical of a maniac but you are aware of your abilities and who you are and how you develop that. It's important to have confidence but also be humble in knowing that at any given moment serious injury can take it all away. That's why you have to have a hand and hand. You have to take advantage of your God-given gifts by playing, but whether you play one, two or 20 years, you have to be prepared for your next career.

It's more important to have a legacy of doing something for a community by creating jobs. It's more important that my legacy be Jimmy King the father, and Jimmy King the businessman, than Jimmy King the basketball player.

During young athletes' introduction to sports during their prep years and beyond, society encourages them to believe that they are the best players on the court and field. We even say, "If you don't believe you're the best, than who else will?" Or if you don't believe you're the best, you will never become a winner or even achieve the ultimate goal of winning, to become a champion. Some of the most successful athletes got there because they did believe they were the best. During the formative years, athletes' egos were developed and these egos became the fuel for their success. But what happens when the ego-driven

> athlete transcends from sports? The cheering stops, but the EGO doesn't. We have created a monster that we now criticize because of ego, instead of using the platform they have created through sports to promote positive charitable causes.

The discussion with Jimmy King was insightful. It leads us to the topic of how collegiate athletes will transition when their sports career come to an end.

Jimmy King's Points to Ponder

- We (the Fab Five) knew that we had a responsibility to others—not just ourselves but to our families and to our communities—to be more than just basketball players and athletes.
- You have to have a Plan B because life is going to deal you different cards that you may not be prepared for.
- It's more important to have a legacy of doing something for a community.

4

WHEN THE CHEERING STOPS

"It is hard to fathom that I am no longer a Missouri football player and the tag and that identity is no longer there." —Jason Ray

When Jason Ray finished his final season with Missouri University football as captain, he found himself without the same status on campus and his feelings are quoted above. This speaks to Eric Erikson's reference to the identity vs. confusion part of the ego. Philanthropy can help address this part of social development.

During my research for this project, I came across the Missouri University's Total Person Program. Director of Life Skills Kimberly Martin was kind enough to do an interview with me.

The mission of the Life Skills program is to inspire student-athletes to continue their pursuit of excellence when the crowd stops cheering. Extensive programming is provided to enhance the overall development of student-athletes as students, citizens and athletes. The five components of the Life Skills program include: Career Development, Community Outreach, Personal Development, Academic Excellence, and Athletic Commitment.

The Total Person Program at Missouri University is dedicated to developing the total student-athlete. Through the program's comprehensive services, Mizzou student-athletes receive top quality assistance to ensure their success. The Total Person Program understands the pressure and special needs of student-athletes and works closely with them to monitor their development and make certain their experience at Mizzou is positive.

The Lifeskills program works with seniors and former student-athletes to provide a network of job opportunities when they have completed their athletic careers. This program provides opportunities and leads for potential careers and jobs once they have finished school. Many employers are looking for competent, competitive and successful employees, and Mizzou student-athletes provide a good match. The program also works with student-athletes to produce and polish outstanding resume and cover letters.

Kim Martin described the program in more detail:

> Our Total Persons Program is the Academic and Life Skills Support Unit for all 500-plus of our student-athletes. The academic side focuses on the academic life of the athlete so schedules, peer mentors, eligibility, and all of that. My piece of the puzzle is with the life skills and career development. Personal development, community service and the largest part is their career development.

Students are becoming more and more receptive to the program as it becomes part of our culture at Mizzou. So they are coming in and getting the help and understanding that they need to start looking toward their future.

We have had this program in place four years now so we have had at least one class go through the entire thing. It's becoming something where the upperclassmen understand why it's important and they are sharing the importance to their underclassmen teammates, explaining why it's necessary to start a resume and why they need to participate in our program. This is from our leadership as well.

The realization of the need for this program evolved over the years. We have had Life Skills and other career programs in our department for quite awhile. It just became evident that we needed to ensure we were providing as much support for students' graduation from Mizzou as we do for their entrance into Mizzou. We wanted to make sure we were providing that support for them.

I would advise incoming students, high school students, to get involved. They need to be involved in their communities, and involved in their schools. Student-athletes need to do more than sports. They should take a leadership role and learn more about themselves. Start figuring out some career areas that might be of interest to them. Shadow professionals to get a feel of what's available and potentially interesting.

We never squash anyone's dream to play at the next level, but we always talk about if that doesn't work, they need a backup plan. They need to understand how to best be prepared for all of their options.

Our athletes also have a huge role in community service and philanthropy. They obviously have a very captive audience. They command a lot of attention just because of what they do in their sport and who they are. I feel they need to use that to give back. Someone helped them get where they are along the way and they need to use that position to be a positive role models. There are a lot of eyes looking at them.

Unfortunately so many of our student-athletes don't take advantage of all the resources available to them. Whether it's because of their youth, lack of time, or failure to understand that they're going to need to make that transition eventually. When our alums return, they often confess that they wish they would have been more involved in the services and resources we provide.

However, those student-athletes who do take advantage of all these valuable resources find the transition much easier. Many of our athletes have gone on to work for companies and are moving up on the leadership ladder. Many have gone on to graduate school and are doing amazing research. We most definitely have many success stories of athletes who have done everything the right way and taken advantage of everything and now are very successful on their chosen path.

LAUREN "LADY" AITCH

"There is a biblical reference that talks about 'seedtime and harvest.' To me that means regardless of your financial state or how you're doing, you always have the ability to act."
—Lauren Aitch

Lauren "Lady" Aitch (pronounced H) began playing basketball in junior high school and played during her years at Waverly High School in Lansing, Michigan. Her team won the state championship in 2005, the only women's team with that title from Waverly High. She committed to Michigan State during her senior year after visits to Syracuse and Michigan. She was supposed to fly out to Auburn and other schools but had already made her decision.

She shares why she wanted to stay in Lansing and go to Michigan State University and what has transpired in her career playing professional basketball.

> My dad, Matthew Aitch, played at Michigan State in the '60s. He was the captain when they won the Big Ten Championship. He was a first-round draft pick. He got drafted to Detroit and was traded to the Pacers. He scored the first two points ever for the Pacers. Unfortunately he passed away during my sophomore year of college. He had an allergic reaction to a medication. However, I

would not have done a lot of the things I've done if he had not passed away. I was always daddy's little girl, and I was always driven and now it gave me an extra-added oomph to do all the things he could not. He was always a mover and shaker. He went overseas and backpacked through Europe, so I wanted to go to Europe. He was one of the first blacks to get a masters degree from Michigan State, so I got my masters. I finished my masters before I went overseas. It's in Public Relations and my undergrad is in Advertising and Science.

I had some great years at MSU. During the season in which I was playing some of the best basketball I ever played, we had a coaching change, I tore my ACL, and my dad passed away. My mom says you have to always keep moving and going forward. If you get stagnant then that is when things catch up to you. If you allow yourself to remain in your misery, you're not going to get anything done. So the challenges made me work harder.

While in my masters program, I became involved in celebrity charity events around Lansing. I also had a philanthropy class, which gave a history of philanthropy, how to set up different sponsorship levels, and the major impact that it can have.

After my dad passed away, I always had it in my mind that I wanted to do a philanthropic organization in memory of him and his name. When I was over in Copenhagen, I reached out to Dr. James Potchen at MSU and gave him my idea. I wanted to have a fashion show featuring former athletes as a charity event. I got out my pen and pad, started drawing, and created my Lady Aitch clothing line.

Dr. Potchen asked what cause I wanted to support. He suggested that I focus on cancer because everyone is touched by cancer in some way. So I chose to focus on preventive forms of stopping cancer. Dr. Potchen says that cancer kills people in many cases because it can't be detected. So the Aitch Foundation is the only charity to ever donate money to MSU Health Teams. Money will also be allocated to early detection devices for all cancers. We are not going to discriminate; we are looking for all cancers. This was all rolled out at The Hidden Key Fashion Show.

My philanthropic work is aided by me being a hometown girl and one of the few women doing this type of activity. So many people, including young girls, know who I am, so why not use my influence for a good thing?

Financially, I'm not at a place where I can do everything I want, but I'm not letting that stop me from having an impact. I'll get a little spiritual on you. There is a biblical reference that talks about "seedtime and harvest." To me that means regardless of your financial state or how you're doing, you always have the ability to act.

I feel like my life is a testimony and those people who have testimonials about giving back need to tell those stories. They need to go speak to kids. If kids don't see you there doing it yourself, they are going to wonder why they should do it.

You don't have to be a professional athlete or celebrity to make a difference. I want to have a mentoring program called 45 Reasons. I wore the number 45 when I played and so did my dad. As adults we sometimes don't think about what's going on in a kid's life. I want to pull out leaders in the high schools and have them mentor each other. There are a couple leaders in every school. We teach them to be the mentors. Sometimes we wear our mentors out. My idea is to have a regenerative process so you can have mentors that come through and replace others. Then they will graduate and go on to help others. There will always be mentors coming through. Also with my foundation I really want to tap in to all the athletes we have at Michigan State to get them out to talk to the kids and help with mentoring. My website is www.aitchfoundation.com and I have LadyAitch.com, which is my fashion line.

Lauren Aitch Points to Ponder:

- Regardless of your financial state or how you're doing, you always have the ability to act
- If kids don't see you there doing it yourself, they're going to wonder why they should do it
- You don't have to be a professional athlete to make a difference

Good People—Horatio Williams

"With hard work you can achieve anything but you have to believe in your greatness."
—Horatio Williams

Achieving through obstacles...that's Horatio Williams. Nearly losing his life in college after being hit by a drunk driver, Horatio Williams battled back from a coma and broken bones with the same tenacity that was instilled in him as a youth on the playing fields of the Eastside of Detroit.

Growing up, Horatio played basketball and football with the Eastside Center and Butzel Middle School. His basketball prowess led him to a college scholarship at Tuskegee University.

Horatio Williams credits Mr. Foster, his Eastside Colts coach, as his inspirational role model. Mr. Foster taught Williams a philosophy to live by, "With hard work you can achieve anything but you have to believe in your greatness."

After his long recovery, Williams went to work for a transportation firm in Michigan owned by his mentor. When the business was closing, his mentor encouraged him to start his own medical transportation firm. He lent Williams the start-up capital and three vehicles and referred a few clients.

In 1992, Horatio Williams formed On Time Transportation Inc., a non-emergency medical transportation firm that provides

24/7 service for clients suffering various injuries. Horatio notes, "The obstacles of my accident led me to this business and it's been a blessing."

With 17 vehicles, he has serviced over 3000 clients and employed 32 people. He went from signing autographs as a college basketball star to signing checks…helping people provide for their families. "While I still miss playing basketball," says Horatio, "working with my clients and providing jobs has been an honor and I thank God for the opportunity."

He established the Horatio Williams Foundation, which has provided additional charitable contributions to the community. In April he sponsors the "Second Chance Basketball Game" so high school seniors who did not receive college scholarships have an opportunity to play in front of scouts and coaches from across the country.

In June, he sponsors a free two-week basketball camp for over 100 youth. In August, he sponsors a free trip to Cedar Point Amusement Park for over 400 youth. In September, he sponsors a back-to-school uniform clothing drive to provide school clothing for underprivileged youth.

Williams is determined to expand his youth outreach, provide more programs, and reach more kids. He is currently working on providing academic (tutorial) assistance to those students needing additional help in all subjects and ACT/SAT testing preparation. As he says, "Life is about learning and I believe kids can achieve their greatness if they are given an opportunity…it's my responsibility to provide them with a chance." Learn more about his foundation at www.horatiowilliamsfoundation.org. Horatio Williams provides an extraordinary example of what an impact former student-athletes can make once the cheering stops. We spoke about how he was originally introduced to philanthropy.

> My mentor, Saunders Dorsey, really educated me about how giving back is really the right thing to do whether you're successful or not. You have to help other people. So I give all the credit to Saunders Dorsey and the things that he instilled in me. He gave me an opportunity to take a transportation company of two vehicles up to 17 vehicles and to be able to help people provide for their families.
>
> Being from the Eastside of Detroit off Van Dyke and Kercheval, every night I used to wish for someone to give me the opportunity to get out of the rut I was in. I didn't want to make any bad decisions; I didn't want anything wrong; I always wanted to do the right thing. I was really blessed and always thought that with hard work you can achieve anything, but you have to believe in your greatness.
>
> One way we help kids is the Second Chance Game. Five or six years ago, a buddy invited me to a basketball game in the Detroit Public Schools. When I started going to the games, I saw a couple kids that we knew from the neighborhood. The next season after they had graduated, I thought they were going to college but I would see them in the stands. I asked why they were not going to college. They responded, "I didn't get a scholarship" or "I didn't get a look," or "I couldn't pass the test." As you know by today's paper, basketball talent is down

in Michigan. So I thought about what I could do to make a difference. That's when we came up with the Second Chance Game. We invited all college scouts to come out from junior colleges, Division III and up. Let's give the players an opportunity to develop into young men and see what it's really about out here in the real world. That's how I developed into a young man. When I went off to school, there was no help. It was like you were in survival mode; you had to take care of your business. People who were successful were able to leave home and make adjustments.

A lot of our kids can't make adjustments. Living in Detroit, there is so much going on. We're known as The Motor City, Motown. We have access to a lot of things that other cities don't have. So when you go down to Alabama and see cotton fields, it's going to be a shock. You go to South Dakota and see bears, it's going to be a shock when you're used to seeing squirrels and dogs.

I always was an entrepreneur. I always was going to find a way. Once I got down to school, I knew my mother was not going to send me any money so I started a t-shirt selling team. This was when Guess Jeans were really popular. So the shirt said, "You don't have to Guess-Tuskegee University." We shopped it around to all the black colleges so during Homecoming we were jamming!

In addition to making the transition, student-athletes have to surround themselves with the right people. The problem that most pro athletes and those going on to the next level have is that they really don't have someone around them who will be honest and tell them the truth that they will listen to.

When I was growing up, my mentor had the top black law firm in the country called Bill and Hudson. Everyone listened to them. They had Muhammad Ali, Larry Holmes, and Don King. They had everybody. Times have changed. Our kids run from us and bypass us and go to who has the most money. Sometimes money is not knowledge. Money is a quick fix.

My proudest philanthropic moment was opening the Horatio Williams facility, because now I can house all of my projects. The worst thing you want to do is have a program but not have anywhere to take it. Now whatever project I believe in I can do because I have a facility. I always wanted to have a facility where I can help by reaching back. This is something like the center I came from—the Eastside Center—which is no longer in existence. If I wasn't home, my mom knew I was at the Eastside Center. It was a safe haven for the youth. If people needed to go shopping, they could send their kids to the Eastside Center. I always wanted to do something like that so a kid would be able to address his or her issues and talents. At this building we plan on having arts, dance, reading classes.

We are still working on the name, whether it will be a complex or campus. We have 35,000 square feet. We have a 400-seat auditorium in the basement. We have a 270-seat banquet hall. We have a 3,000 square-foot commercial kitchen. We have 18 office spaces. This was previously the Wayne State Medical Society.

We have a huge event taking place here. The 2011 NFL Defensive Rookie of the Year, Detroit Lion Ndamukong Suh, has a family foundation that is hosting a Guinness World Record event here.

This is great opportunity for the Horatio Williams Foundation and a great opportunity for this community. A lot of times pro athletes go to the suburbs or go to different areas. Out this window you see Ford Field, Comerica Park, Crain Communication, the General Motors building and all of downtown Detroit. In the early years they used to call this area Paradise Valley. So there is some history here. This area is almost 90% occupied. So now we are bringing more life over here. There is probably only 10% of Detroit that is 90% occupied.

Our mission with the foundation is to make sure we have a lot of activities for the kids during the week and on the weekend. Even if we're just showing the latest movie. Maybe we can work something out where we can show the latest movie in the theater. With gas prices being up, people shouldn't have to travel to go to the movie theater. If we have something in the community people know they could walk to, they would do it.

It's important for student-athletes to remember, regardless of your walk of life, you can reach back and help somebody. Let your spirits go out to the universe where everyone doesn't have this negative thought of robbing and stealing. Get out there and work for yours and your blessings will come. Just have the right spirit. Have something that motivates you. I had an opportunity to play pro basketball but the greatest feeling for me now is knowing I can help people provide for their families.

It's important to use your pro or celebrity platform to help others. It's a great feeling because everyone needs to be a part of something. We all are competitive by nature. We all are part of some team. I still deal with guys that I grew up playing football and basketball with. Because we were part of something, we did everything we could to help each other like family. We wanted the best for each other; we wanted to win because we never had anything.

This idea is lost on the next generation because the problems we run into today revolve around everyone being driven by money. People want to know how they can benefit, instead of just being a part of something.

Young people have to find something that they love and they won't care about getting paid. That's the key.

HORATIO WILLIAMS POINTS TO PONDER

- Giving back is really the right thing to do whether you're "successful" or not.
- Sometimes money is not knowledge. It's just a quick fix.
- Regardless of your walk in life, you can reach back and help somebody.

Greg Kelser

"Work hard and do all you can to try to make it happen but also understand you have to have something else." —Greg Kelser

I had the pleasure of meeting Greg Kelser almost 20 years ago. This was after he had already reached fame and stardom as a standout player alongside "Magic" Earvin Johnson at Michigan State University. Greg Kelser is a native Detroiter and we are both alums of Henry Ford High School. Greg had a vending machine business in Henry Ford. Not only is he an entrepreneur, he is a philanthropist as well. He provided scholarships to students at Henry Ford through the proceeds of his business. When I graduated in 1993, I applied for and received one of those coveted scholarships. Of course this made me very familiar with Greg Kelser. Over the years we kept in contact. In his role as television color commentator for the Detroit Pistons, we reconnected while I had an internship there. Since then I have stayed in touch and was happy to return the favor and assist when he requested sponsorship for his basketball camp at Grosse Pointe South High School. It was his fourth week of basketball camp, with the first three being at Detroit Renaissance High School and he and I enjoyed a conversation about sports and philanthropy.

In the summer I like to have basketball camps, which is something I started in 1978. Obviously basketball camps do cost. You're not going to get facilities free. You're not going to be able to come in and have people work for a whole week, six or seven hours a day, and not pay them so we do have some costs involved. So we set what we feel is a fair price for our kids to participate. Even with that, there are kids in the community that cannot afford basketball camps. So a long time ago it became my endeavor to try to make this opportunity available to more kids. So through the efforts of kind organizations like yours we were able to get some of those dollars to put into the camp and give the kids this experience. And I can tell you from all indications the kids really, really appreciate it and they embrace it. They know it's something they are very fortunate to be able to engage in.

Growing up, I didn't come from an affluent family. My mom and dad worked really hard. My dad was in the Air Force and my mom worked in various employment considerations. They made sacrifices for me to make sure I could have the things that I needed and a lot of the things I wanted as well. I understand that's not always the case for a lot of youngsters. So people have been very kind to me. Along with my parents there have been so many extensions of my parents that have cared about my well-being and my development so I'm just doing my part now because I'm in a position to help others. Even at my age I'm still getting help from people. I think when people see you trying to do different things, they want to help you reach your goals. One of my goals is trying to increase the number of kids I can impact through my basketball camp. It's just about giving back.

With our camps, we provide a week for campers to focus on basketball, but at Renaissance, we have an additional program specific to the City of Detroit. I had an organization that I partnered with called Winning Futures, which is a mentoring organization. So we were able to use their capabilities to bring in volunteers to mentor these children for 1½ hours every day. So the kids showed up for breakfast, they went into the classroom and we just rotated until everybody had an experience with 25% in the classroom and 75% in the gym. We are just trying to develop the whole person. In my other basketball camps we don't get into the gym until Friday because I give them a homework assignment on Monday that they must carry out before the completion of camp. Every day they get a message about education and how critically important it is in their lives.

We always stress to these kids that they must have more than one plan. We all share with them the fact that when we were their ages we all aspired to be professional athletes. We saw ourselves and envisioned ourselves as that and we didn't care about the odds against us. That's OK. We don't try to douse anyone's dream. Work hard and do all you can to try to make it

> happen but also understand you have to have something else. I'm a prime example. I realized my goal of playing professional basketball would not last forever and I needed to have something to fall back on. I tell the kids that I played professional basketball for six years before an injury short-circuited my career but because I got a good, sound education, I was able to parlay that into a 25-year professional broadcasting career. You tell me what's more important and what's more valuable. Your education. In my case, my second career has been far more long-lasting and sustainable than the first.

You can find out about more of Greg and his great work at www.GregoryKelser.com.

GREG KELSER'S POINTS TO PONDER

- When people see you trying to do different things, they want to help you reach your goals.
- It's important to develop the "whole person."
- You must have more than one plan.

5

The Stage Is Yours

"I wanted to get into education because I felt like I was old enough to still be cool. I know who Lil Wayne is, I know who Young Jeezy is, I have a Twitter account, I have a Facebook page."
—Jalen Rose, ESPN Analyst/
Former NBA and Fab Five Member

Athletes are arguably some of society's most respected, highly regarded and sometimes controversial figures. Tiger, Lebron, Terrelle Pryor, Reggie Bush. All of these individuals have been the focus of our interest for their actions unrelated to the sports they play. Regardless of why they have received our attention, the reality is that they have it. They have been the center of television and Internet discussions. Their actions, right or wrong, captivate us. Their ability to impact brands is evident in the millions of dollars they receive for their endorsements. Terrelle Pryor and his collegiate counterparts can barter goods and services for their own football paraphernalia. The celebrity of athletes consumes America and the world. They have a star power that makes Hollywood envious. They also have an underutilized platform. They can be the catalyst for change in society. They can influence future generations in a way that no other public figures have.

Mike Martin

Mike Martin, no relation to Kim Martin, is an NFL prospect at the University of Michigan. Mike is a perfect example of a student-athlete who is not waiting until he makes it to the pros to be philanthropic. We spoke about why he first became involved in philanthropy.

> I initially entered the realm of philanthropy in high school. All student-athletes at Detroit Catholic Central have mandatory community service hours. As a freshman, this was kind of a burden—I was going out of my way and couldn't hang out with my friends—but after all my teammates got together down in Detroit going to soup kitchens and helping out in churches, we all started to realize that it was fun. Not only that but we could feel that we were having an impact on the people we were around. That was huge and that was really how it all started. From that point on, it's been developing as I have gotten older and have been able to do things on a bigger scale, like going to Michigan and being a football player.
>
> Many of my college teammates are just getting introduced to philanthropy now. A lot of my guys went to public schools and weren't exposed to community

service. I think when you're younger you really don't think about other people. You're trying to get yourself right, which is understandable.

It's sometimes difficult; once I was speaking to a group in a hospital and became really nervous. It was the summer of 2010 and I was asking myself, 'As a young guy, what do I have to give? What do they want to hear from me? What do I have to offer?' I felt like I really didn't have much to say, but being in the position that I am and getting a degree at Michigan and doing well and being successful, it was important to those guys. Them being able to see me giving back and hanging out with them meant a lot.

At first philanthropy was mandatory, but now it's something I do on my own. I just do things as simple as going to youth football camps or going to Mott Hospital with my teammates. Even on fan day, it's the smallest thing that means the most. Not just signing something but finding the little kid in the corner who's quiet and shy and going to hang out with him. I feel like philanthropy can be on a bunch of different levels and there are different types. I know just doing that, that little kid will remember that moment for the rest of his life.

At this point in my career, philanthropy isn't at all about spending money—it's totally passion driven and all about spending time with others.

Our coach, Brady Hoke, is so passionate about philanthropy and he exudes his passion when he talks about it. With the hospital visit, he got excited, jumped around, and said, "Let's get a bus and go down there and hang out with some kids!"

That enthusiasm in turn excited all of us; my teammates were wide-eyed like, "Man, Coach Hoke is really into it."

At the University of Michigan, I don't feel like a lot of guys originally looked at philanthropy as being important or wanted to go out and do extra things outside of football. I think on my team, many of the players have changed and they are taking on more outside of football. They realize that just because they are from another part of the country, they're now flipping the lens and looking at it from the outside in. They're seeing that they can give back to someone who was just like me because they are role models.

When you're at the University of Michigan, everything is on a much larger scale. You meet so many people from all over and realize different parts of life. It's a great place to be.

In terms of future plans and philanthropic goals, I'm working with my close friends Chris Fischer and Ryan Doyle to create Forever Legit. It's an idea that Chris brought to me a year ago. We want to be able to travel around the country and impact people's lives in a major way. We want to collaborate with professional athletes, their media outlets, and foundations that they already have. We want to siphon the energy from the game of football and pump it back into the cities.

MIKE MARTIN'S POINTS TO PONDER

- Philanthropy can be on a bunch of different levels and there are different types.
- Philanthropy isn't all about spending money—it's totally passion driven and all about spending time with others.
- We (Forever Legit) want to siphon the energy from the game of football and pump it back into cities.

Nick Vandenbosch—
Is there a Doctor in the house?

Nick Vandenbosch is from Muskegon, Michigan, where he attended Orchardview High School. After high school, he went to Adrian College, where he played football for four years, and then medical school at Michigan State's College of Osteopathic Medicine.

He discussed how his background prepared him for his interest in philanthropy.

> My high school was middle class so we had a lot of different people from different cultures in that neighborhood. It helped mold who I am. In college I continued to meet a lot of different people from different backgrounds. At Adrian not only did I play varsity football, which was a great experience, but I also got my bachelors in biology with a minor in chemistry. Then I went to medical school, where I was trained as a regular doctor but there was additional training in medical techniques based on a holistic approach.
>
> Playing professional or semi-professional football was always in the back of my mind. I knew I wanted to be involved in some area of sports. I was high school valedictorian so I took my studies pretty seriously and I knew early on I wanted to go to medical school. It came down to either going to medical school or continuing to play football. As I was going into my sophomore year of college I blew my hamstring out. I

fought hard and came back from the injury but never really got the look that I had hoped for. I battled back and at the end of my senior year there were some arena football teams that were interested in having me play for them and go workout and tryout. My good friend Terrence Williams ended up playing arena football and then going to law school.

The WV Foundation is a nonprofit organization that Terrence and I started with the focus of giving opportunities to high school graduates We do this by giving out scholarships and starting the Muskegon All-Star Classic football game. It gives seniors who graduated a chance to perform in front of their community one last time. They also will become eligible for a number of scholarships from the proceeds and advertising dollars from the event.

Even though this is the last time they will be playing, they can still get scholarships and have some fun. We will also be reaching out to scouts and colleges that don't quite have their rosters set. So the students may have an additional opportunity to get recruited.

When Terrence and I first got to college and were in training camp, we heard other guys talk about how they were involved in an all-star game. This was in Macomb and Wayne Counties in Metro-Detroit. Terrence and I said that we wish we had something like that. So we had this idea for a while and we knew somehow we wanted to give back. Now that Terrence has finished law school and I medical school, we figure that we can either keep talking about it or finally put in some work and get this thing accomplished. So we started the non-profit organization in October 2011 and now we are just moving ahead with a full head of steam.

The message I would want to get across is that if you can dream and believe in something, you can make it happen. That is not only in sports, it's in academics, relationships, and helping your community. The Muskegon All-Star Classic embodies all of those things. It will take place on June 16th and will be a clean, fun event for the community.

The WV foundation is not strictly for student-athletes. Looking big picture, we want to do internships for kids so that they can see things outside of Muskegon or outside of Detroit. Also, we want to promote health fairs and health screenings.

You can keep up with us on Facebook at Muskegon All-Star Classic and twitter @muskegonclassic.

Technology and Philanthropy

Each spring, thousands of high school seniors face one of the hardest decisions of their lives. For a small portion of America's graduating seniors, the pressure surrounding that decision takes on a whole new meaning. Elite high school athletes, who in previous decades were merely jocks at their local high school, have now become state and nationwide celebrities.

This transformation can be attributed to the growth in popularity of college sports and continued advancements in media technology. The Internet has made it possible for college sports fans to familiarize themselves with their favorite school's recruits before they ever step foot on campus. Multiple websites are dedicated to collecting information on the physical attributes, athletic performance, and potential college choices of high school athletes. The past five years have produced a plethora of highly publicized prep media events, ranging from nationally televised high school basketball games watched by millions of people to nationally televised press conferences held by high school recruits for the purpose of publicly announcing their schools of interest. Due to the increasing interest in elite high school prospects, the nature of reporting college recruiting has changed in recent years. College town and major city newspapers now designate pages of their sports sections to elite recruits. Naturally, the essence of that reporting changes dramatically depending on the market of the newspaper.

Video games have provided another platform that increases the notoriety and popularity of amateur athletes. Although their names are not mentioned in college basketball and football games like NCAA Football 11, the students' likenesses are used. I'm not here to discuss the merits of paying college players, however I will argue that the debate itself speaks to the validity behind the fact that these "amateur" athletes are truly nationally and even internationally recognized sports figures with a following and a potential platform that can impact social change.

Let's not keep our heads in the sand on this issue. Amateur athletes are the driving force behind a billion-dollar industry—college sports. This is all the more reason why these student-athletes need to be exposed to philanthropy now—to have a major impact on social change for future generations.

Pros and Cons of athlete notoriety and social media

Social media will play an ever-increasing role in the lives of athletes. The next group of current and former professional athletes has a strong social media presence—Twitter, Facebook, etc.—that they use to promote their philanthropic efforts. They represent a future of sports, technology, and philanthropy.

Athletes use social media for marketing and endorsements, but what about using it for philanthropy? Shaquille O'Neal claims he's the most dominant player in NBA history, but few would argue he's the best tweeter the league ever produced. With over three million followers, he's leveraged the platform (and really, all of the Internet) as well as anyone.

"CHILD PLEASE"—OCHOCINCO

Ochocinco, formerly Chad Johnson and now a member of the New England Patriots, is one of the most popular NFL players as well as being a pop culture icon. Much of this notoriety can be credited to this Pro-Bowler's style of play, but some is attributed to his social networking dominance. Ochocinco is approaching three million Twitter followers. As ESPN's Amy K. Nelson's January 2010 article points out, in the past, if a fan wanted to reach a professional athlete, there were generally only two routes: either a personal connection or pen and paper. If you wrote a letter to a superstar athlete, it probably would be one of thousands in a bag that would never be seen or read.

Now, technology and social-networking sites have dramatically changed the landscape of fan and player relationships. Unfortunately, an example of this was made evident by the tragic death of one of Ochocinco's biggest fans. Chris Kernich, a 23-year-old college student, was the victim of a fatal beating after which he was clinging to life in the hospital. While he was in a coma, doctors informed Chris's family that he could hear them. In order to inspire Chris to awaken, his family and friends thought of different ways to help Chris. They created a Facebook page that grew to include over 3,000 people. They sent the following Tweets to Ochocinco to see if he could call or visit to help Chris come out of the coma:

@OGOchoCinco URGENT!! — We are asking for some of your support to help @the_man_CK survive this hard time. This would mean so much! PLZRE-SPOND — Nov. 19, 2009: Twitter message from Kernich's friend Katrina Polansky

@OGOchoCinco Chad please come visit my friend Chris Kernich at Akron City Hospital. He suffered a bad head injury and he is your #1 Fan!! — Nov. 19, 2009: Twitter message from Kernich's friend Zack Siegrist

After seeing Twitter posts that one of his biggest fans was in critical condition, Ochocinco called Chris when a coach approached him with the family's contact information. It was too late. Chris had died and he was buried in an Ochocinco jersey. The family was grateful that Ochocinco had taken the time to call. He dedicated the next game between the Cincinnati Bengals and the Cleveland Browns, which was on the same day as Chris's funeral, to Chris.

While scanning his Twitter feed, Ochocinco spotted a message from one of Chris Kernich's closest friends Kirk Stivers that read:

@ogochocinco @the_man_CK was buried today with your jersey! A great person was laid to rest today. His memory will always be alive! RIP CK

Less than five minutes after Stivers posted the message, he saw a return message that made his jaw drop and tears start to stream. Ochocinco had a message for Chris Kernich:

@the_man_CK bruh I love you man, RIP, you'll never be forgotten, I'm playing for you tomorrow

Prior to the tweets, Chris's sister Chelsea Groom was not a fan of Ochocinco because she felt he was "too flashy." The Bengals won the game and Ochocinco won their hearts.

As sad as this story ends, this does not mean that every star athlete will and should respond to all social media requests. In defense of the athlete (or anyone for that matter), that's an unrealistic expectation. However, this is just one of countless stories that speaks to the emotional impact social networking can have when athletes use it positively. Through smart phones, tablets, and other technology tools, social media is the medium many live by and will be using as a key form of communicating positive messaging and philanthropic messages in the future.

Tweetup for a Cause—Ndamukong Suh

Another Pro-Bowler, Ndamukong Suh, has used social media and Twitter for a great cause as well when he utilized a "Tweetup."

A Tweetup, according to *PC Magazine*, is a "gathering of users brought together by Twitter." However, in Ndamukong's case, it's inviting fans, via his Twitter account, to hang out, win prizes and participate in a live Q&A. Ndamukong set his first Guinness World Record in Lincoln, Nebraska by hosting a Tweetup at his alma mater before the 2011 University of Nebraska Spring Football Game on April 18, 2011. The previous record of 1,149 was set by Ford Motor Company and in Nebraska, 1,935 people gathered to crush that record.

Ndamukong's Suh successful attempt in breaking a Guinness World Record generated not only local media in Nebraska but national attention including mentions in *USA Today*, ESPN, MSN, Fox News, *Detroit Free Press* and the official @Twitter account.

In July of 2011 he attempted to break his own record in Detroit, and I'm proud to say that I personally was involved in this attempt. Unfortunately the abrupt conclusion of the NFL lockout posed scheduling challenges so Ndamukong was not able to attend and we didn't break the record. His event still was a major accomplishment in itself for several reasons. It took place at the Horatio Williams Foundation's new location, giving it great exposure to the community, and media and vendor fees supported his charity. The community was also treated to free fun and games throughout the day. This all was driven through Twitter and social media.

Using social media as a platform also created publicity for the Ndamukong Suh Family Foundation, which focuses on Education, Health, Wellness and Nutrition, and International Outreach. Learn more about their extraordinary work at www.Suhfoundation.org.

What I found to be an interesting contrast between the Lincoln, Nebraska and Detroit, Michigan Tweetups was familiarity. Lincoln is a college town where most students are familiar with Twitter or have a Twitter account themselves (according to a Ypulse Research study in 2010, 42% of teens and college students use Twitter). So the idea of attending a Tweetup for your favorite native son is not foreign. However, when the idea was introduced to Detroit, the first question for many was, "What's a Tweetup?" This was a totally new concept to many Detroiters and understandably so.

The don dada of social media is Mark Zuckerburg's Facebook. It began in a dorm room at Harvard University and was initially meant to be an elite and exclusive network amongst college students. For many users Twitter is an evolution from Facebook. The great thing about Ochocinco and Ndamukong (what names, huh?) using social media as a medium to promote charity (or themselves) is they become social media ambassadors and are introducing this platform to many who might never otherwise have a Twitter account or attend a Tweetup.

As we look at the impact of Facebook, which has more than 750 million users, we should accept that these forms of social media are here to stay, and they will become increasingly more instrumental in promoting messaging, to include the powerful message of philanthropy.

Todd “TJ” Duckett—Living in Truth

“A single raindrop creates a flood. To me, the people are the flood. It’s the people that make the change.”
—TJ Duckett

Todd “TJ” Duckett attended Michigan State University, and is recognized as one of the greatest football players in MSU’s history. Todd enjoyed a successful seven-year career as an NFL running back. His bio states that “Football was something I did for fun, not what defined me. I want to help change a person’s life, directly, and that’s where I find my joy.”

Todd created the TD Foundation while he was playing football. Losing his mother to cancer at an early age sparked a lifelong interest in cancer research. Through the TD Foundation, he reached out to those living with cancer to help them live as cancer survivors rather than cancer victims. Later, he moved on to co-found an organization called Lunch with a Purpose to encourage others to support local area charities and nonprofits by making contributions of personal time and effort, as well as monetary donations and fund-raising assistance. Todd also is a mentor for The Turning Point of Lansing, Transforming Boys to Men.

When I sat down with Todd we talked about a number of things. But we started with the topic of “People needing to live in Truth.” I asked him to talk about that more.

Me being a former athlete, I can help others by talking very candidly about the things that I went through. That slowly became my purpose. A single raindrop creates a flood. To me, the people are the flood. It's not water. This is a new mindset and a new way of thinking. It's the people who make the change. When I go talk to kids, I tell my story. I talk of my depression. I used to go out and spend $2, 3, 4, 5 grand on a Friday night and not even remember the next day. That amount can give so many people a mortgage or rent for the month. So to whom much is given, much is required. At 21 and 22 years of age, I didn't see that. I don't think anyone would see it at that age. Once I got back to Lansing, Michigan, I started seeking more and looking for more, I started to volunteer. The more I started to volunteer, the more I realized how tough it is out here. I saw how families could live off some of the money that I would blow on a Friday night to some club owners who are not doing anything for the community. So I said if that's the case, let's shut it down. Let's pump the brakes. I don't believe in giving someone money and walking away. I want to do it in a way in which they can have sustained income. I adopted a school and I go in there and I ask, "What do you guys need?" They say we need basketballs; we need jerseys. Sure. I can bring it to you tomorrow. But sometimes it can mean being present to volunteer and tutor. Just showing up.

Student-athletes and high school and collegiate

standouts need to find out why they play the game. Do you play the game because you love it? Do you play the game because you're good and you can make some money? Do you play the game because it gives you status? Why do you play the game? If you understand why you play the game, that will dictate your next steps. If you play the game for money, eventually you will get cut. If you play the game for money, that means you want to spend it when you have it so you're going to lose it. So that means that you're going to be cut and be broke at the same time if you just play for money.

I played the game because I loved football. I enjoyed it up until the minute I start seeing it as a business. Once I saw how the whole business side worked, I retired.

When I see my former football colleagues, some of them understand my decision to quit, but it's hard to really understand unless you have been removed from the situation and you're still getting those five- and six-figure checks every other week that some of these guys get paid. As a 20-something in the professional sports environment, there is an image. I was 21, a first-round draft choice in Atlanta. Believe it or not, you get caught up in that image and try to live it.

Other athletes may have difficulty trying to escape the image that is portrayed of them. That's why I come back to saying it's about finding out your truth. Your truth is who you see when you look in the mirror. I did this exercise with myself. There was no coaching involved. I went into a room, turned off all the lights, and I was meditating—praying and asking myself tough questions. It's just me, myself, and I in the room and here I am making excuses for the questions. I wasn't giving myself straight answers. If I'm doing that, how do I expect to bring an effective message to other people's lives? It did a lot for me. It helped me stop fearing taking risks.

My occupation as a football player hindered me in a way because of what I have; I didn't want to lose money or material goods. I look at other go-getters and what they have; they're fighting to get $1000, they're fighting to get seed money for their start-up company. On the other hand, I may have that $10,000 or $20,000 to start a business. But I would say that I am not going to start the business because I don't want to risk losing the money.

It's tough hearing everything everyone else is going to say because 75% of athletes go broke three years after playing. So if I'm taking risks and I don't know exactly what I'm doing, I might be in that same category. And of course I don't want to be in that category. I think part of that fear of risk prevented me from finding my true passion.

It's scary. This journey started for me a year ago at age 29. It was a time in my life when I realized I wanted more. The transition from football was a depressing time for me. I got caught up in things too much and I was blowing it. I believed that there had to be more. I didn't like where I was at. One reason I stopped playing was because I lost the love. I saw the Players Club. You remember that line, "Make the money, don't let the money make you."

Many other athletes are undoubtedly in that same space, not knowing what they want to do or where they want to be. That's one of the reasons I'm back in school now. I was feeling a lack of purpose and wasn't sure what my future was going to be. Since I was eight years old, football was my life. In season, out of season, it was always there.

A year ago I had a vision that I wanted to start a school and teach some of these kids up-to-date information. I wanted to buy a school here in Lansing. I got about 11 people together. People were into it but there really was not a lot they were trying to do to make it happen. Then there were a lot of red tape issues. It was expensive. Things just fell apart. I then found out that for $12,000 I could buy a school in Africa for a whole year as opposed to spending $800,000 here in the United States that would still need renovations and other work. I did that, visited them and stayed in touch with them. I now have a school in Arusha, Tanzania through the Make A Difference Tanzania Foundation. I have 62 kids there ages six to eight years old. My long-term goal for the foundation is to have a platform that can affect anyone from middle school to 80 years old by helping them find their self worth and realizing what type of impact they can have on their community. This is for the people who don't know who they are or why they are here. Following the crowd, you're never going to find your reality.

You can learn more about Todd "TJ" Duckett and his great work at www.newworldflood.org.

TJ Duckett's Points to Ponder

- If you understand why you play the game, that will dictate your next steps.
- Make the money; don't let the money make you.
- If you follow the crowd, you're never going to find your reality.

6

COACHING CHARACTER

"And if God has given you a lot of ability, I believe you should be held to a higher level of expectation."
—Tony Dungy

College Coaching Character

College coaches play a unique role in this process. They are looked up to and respected by high school and AAU (Amateur Athletic Union) coaches. Just like professional athletes, with this type of admiration and notoriety, college coaches have a platform. And let's not kid ourselves. Some college coaches walk on water at their respective colleges and universities. Some have more name recognition than their college or university president, and a select few could challenge the governor of their state for the top spot. With that, are coaches really leveraging their status in a way that can benefit students off the court or playing field?

Philanthropy and community service is approached differently throughout society and by different cultures. It's almost taboo to talk about the charitable work you do. However, I think we need to rethink that approach as it relates to promoting philanthropic principles to future generations. How can they be what they cannot see? More importantly, a coach or athlete being an advocate of philanthropy does not necessarily mean they are giving constant shameless plugs to their good works.

Summers are a unique time for college coaches and recruits. It's when the coaches travel the country watching AAU games. They can scout their prospects but cannot talk to them. Players scan the stands to see who's there watching them. What's going on is completely understood by the players, parents, and coaches. My concern is that this practice only emphasizes a student-athlete going on to play in college and possibly the professional ranks. However there is no emphasis on any other personal development and life skills, like becoming involved in community service and philanthropy. It couldn't hurt, and could greatly help, if college coaches held a forum for high school coaches to emphasize the importance of having well-rounded recruits. One example of making the recruits more well rounded is exposing them to community service and philanthropy. If the advantages of character building and integrity can be promoted, coaches on all levels will see this benefit. The students will be the ultimate winners because they would receive information about something that can help them regardless of their success in sports. They will know that with philanthropy, everyone wins.

Maurice Menefee

"I marched with Dr. King and some of his traits rubbed off on me."

—Maurice Menefee

Maurice Menefee was born in Tuskegee, Alabama and received a scholarship to Florida A&M University. He was the first of his family to go to college. He eventually transferred to Alabama A&M and graduated with a Bachelor of Science. Basketball delivered him from his meager beginning to where he is now. He played basketball in the United States, New Zealand, Australia and Puerto Rico. He always wanted to work with young men and help develop them into outstanding people.

He spoke about the importance of being a role model.

> My immediate family didn't play basketball; they didn't play any sports. I didn't have a role model pushing me. The more I got into it the more I wanted to continue, and not having anyone to push me like that made me want to do something for the next generation of players to help get them moving in the right direction. I had that urge to do that.
>
> I coached basketball at Redford High School for nine years. While coaching and teaching, I saw that what needed to be done athletically and physically and knew I needed to become part of the administration to bring about change. I helped get middle school basketball started in Detroit. I pushed and pushed until I got that

> going. When I got to Henry Ford I wanted all sports to be successful. Not just one. If you can just get one championship in one sport, people seem to be satisfied. I didn't like that. I wanted to get all sports up and running. I'm not one to toot my own horn, but in 2000 we won seven championships in junior varsity football and I don't think that was ever done in Detroit.
>
> Present-day athletes with their million-dollar contracts have an obligation to remember their roots both monetarily as well as giving back with services. Athletes that I helped introduce to basketball went on to have collegiate and professional careers. I would always tell them, "Don't forget your little brothers. You can help them." But unfortunately it didn't work out like that. They could have at least helped the kids with uniforms.
>
> The best coaches can impress upon the players not to forget where they came from and don't forget to give back. You have to give back. I have done it all my life. We have to instill in them to give back.

Coaches at all level of sports have a considerable amount of influence on the personal development of their players on and off the court. Many could argue that some coaches have MORE influence over players than their own parents. This influence is rightfully so in some cases where a young person is born into circumstances of poverty, drugs, and despair. This begs the question if coaches are using this role to encourage student-athletes to be more than just successful players, are they really helping to broaden student-athletes for successful and fulfilled lives, even without going to the next level of the sport they love?

Letters to Coach K and Coach Cal

Coach Mike Krysewski
Duke University
Box 90555
Durham, NC 27708

Coach John Calipari
UK Athletics
Joe Craft Center
338 Lexington Ave
Lexington, KY 40506-0604

Dear Coaches:

Let me begin by complimenting you both on your many accomplishments. Between the two of you, you have national championships and provided the NBA with some of its most talented players. There is no question that you are two of the most influential coaches in NCAA Basketball and arguably all of sports.

You have emphasized the importance of your players' success both on the court and off. That's why in my book *Unlikely Saviors: Realizing the positive impact amateur and professional athletes can have on society through philanthropy*, I am asking for your assistance in a National Call to Action. I believe that your influence on AAU, high school, and college coaches can help promote philanthropy among amateur and professional athletes. I am asking that all coaches at every level of competition take one sanctioned practice day, and instead of a regular practice, have a team community service. This could be the team volunteering at a shelter, assisted living facility, food drive, etc.

Many coaches already promote this type of team building. However, there are many who do not. Also, as you know, the influence that coaches have on their players is so powerful; a coach's introduction to community service can have much more impact on a player. Your encouragement of coaches to promote a Day of Service will internalize a community service experience to athletes in a way they may never have had. Studies show, the earlier a person is introduced to philanthropy, the more s/he will give over a lifetime. Also, as my book discusses, philanthropy can fill the void that develops when athletes transition from their chosen sport.

I hope you can see my vision of using the platform that these amazing athletes have in a way to offer a positive and lasting impact on society. For more information about *Unlikely Saviors*, please go to www.unlikelysaviors.com.

Sincerely,

Lindsay W. Huddleston II
www.lindsayhuddleston.com

Darren Zwick

"Accountability for an athlete is really important. My expectations of my players are to be passionate about what you're doing and accountable as well."

—Darren Zwick

Darren Zwick grew up in Holt, Michigan. He attended Holt High School and was the basketball team's MVP and captain for two years. He went on to play basketball at Olivet College and was a two-time captain there. Leadership has always been important to Darren. After four years of college basketball, he finished as an academic All-American, one of only 15 in the country to have that honor. A magna cum laude graduate now working at the Michigan Dental Association, Darren is the head basketball coach at Lansing Catholic High School. He's been coaching there 13 years and in 2008 his team won the Class B State Championship after being down six out of seven games in the tournament. Darren has also led his team to five straight league titles.

Darren said his most humbling moment was winning the state championship. "Many coaches coach for 30 years and never get on that stage. We did it in Year Five with a good group of kids, good help, and school support. I don't think it's just me. I always like to thank others."

Coach Zwick spoke with me about the role coaches should play in getting their student-athletes involved with philanthropy.

> We need to provide that leadership. In our basketball program we talk about leadership all the time and

how important that is. The motto of our program is "To be passionate about what we do and be accountable about what we do." Passionate and accountable. I try to keep it very simple. And then I explain that. I get in front of the parents and kids and I ask, "What does that mean?" Of course we want you to be passionate about basketball because that's why you're here, but we want you to find other passions. Whether it's in your classroom or your favorite subject. Maybe it is philanthropy. It could be a lot of things.

Accountability for an athlete is really important. Whether they want it or not, they're under the spotlight. Especially in the area of what I call the two major sports. You get publicity. Football and basketball are on the news in the wintertime every Tuesday and Friday. People recognize that and recognize the players. So I always tell them, no matter where you're at, and whether you're wearing a Lansing Catholic shirt or not, people are going to have an impression of you. Are you going to be that punk kid who's running around letting people see you're from Lansing Catholic? People who will then say the Lansing Catholic basketball team is a bunch of punks? Or do you want to be opening doors for people and thanking them and being polite? That's accountability to me in the classroom and in the lunchroom so I try to really explain that expectation to them—to be passionate about what you're doing and accountable as well. That fosters leadership. So to get back to really answering the question, playing basketball is a privilege and they should take that privilege and go out and do community service.

We have done some things over the years like serve food to the underprivileged. Our kids in general at Lansing Catholic do community service. They have service hours and a community service day. They are getting exposed to philanthropy. This school does some wonderful things to foster leadership and set the groundwork for kids to have a philanthropic attitude.

By not just focusing on the sport, we try to create a student-athlete who is more successful in life, not just basketball. This whole-person development helps the game, because it leads to individuals becoming some of the best players who can come from behind and win championships, but it also leads to winners in life beyond basketball.

We obviously have to develop their sport-specific skills. For young kids, confidence is huge for success. No matter what, during a battle, the kids have to have confidence that they can get it done. The confidence must come from their leader.

We stress that our kids are not just accountable for playing basketball. I want our basketball kids to be the leaders in the school. Our basketball guys on game day get dressed up with a shirt and tie. The varsity coach before me started the tradition but I continued it. It was his idea but I love it because when you see a hallway of kids then you see these 12 to 15 kids who are wearing a sports coat and tie, they become leaders. To me that says

I'm going to dress for success today; I'm going to look like a leader; I'm wearing this so I stand out. So I think as a coach we want them to act the right way and perform the right way socially and in the classroom. To me it's just remembering more than a basketball program; they represent a school. They represent their family.

We do have some problems with rebellion, and we have affluent kids coming from stable backgrounds who maybe feel a little entitled to their position as leaders on the team.

My approach is not to embarrass them in front of the kids, but to bring them into my office and talk it through with them. Why did you make that decision in practice? Why did you make the decision to disrespect that teacher? These are the consequences for your behavior.

I witnessed one student where his behavior in the classroom affected his play on the court. When behavior outside of basketball was very inconsistent, the level of play was inconsistent. When he got in trouble in class and was a goofball, it carried into basketball.

Creating philanthropic behavior in these kids is all about the development. Sometimes it works against the more affluent kids because if you come from money, you're used to having material goods. When you're not used to having those things it makes you appreciate what you have more and say all right, this was a gift to me, I want to give back this gift.

Fostering philanthropic behavior begins with the coaches. Coaches at every level are under pressure to win. If they don't win, they won't last very long. They have a line to walk with winning versus their coaching ethics. From a philanthropic standpoint, in my mind they do have the time. They're not recruiting 24/7. During the day they have a lot of time. They watch a lot of film but they have assistants around them to help. I really believe that if they wanted to spend more time with philanthropic work, it would make a tremendous difference because of the high profile role that they're in. I think that some of them do, whether they set up their own charities or are part of other groups. I know Coach Izzo and Coach Dantoni (Michigan State basketball and football respectively) send their kids over to Lansing Catholic. They're involved in the Miracle Network and other charities.

DARREN ZWICK POINTS TO PONDER

- Of course we want you to be passionate about basketball, but we want you to find other passions.
- Playing basketball is a privilege and players should take that privilege and go out and do community service.
- A "whole-person" development helps the game, because it leads to individuals becoming some of the best players who can come from behind and win championships, but it also leads to winners in life beyond basketball.

7

The Power of Philanthropy

"If professional athletes and entertainers can convince the public to buy sneakers and perfume by the truckload, why not use that same power to promote charitable giving?"
—Stephanie Sandler, The Giving Back Fund

Stephanie Sandler has been with The Giving Back Fund since June of 1999. She has provided philanthropic consulting and management for more than 75 professional athletes and entertainers. These clients include Yao Ming, Jalen Rose, Elton Brand, Darren and Jamie Sharper, Antwaan Randel El, Ben Roethlisberger, Ben Gordon, Scott Mellanby, Pearl Sinn-Bonanni, Sam Madison, Nancy Kerrigan, Kenyon Martin, and Jamie-Lynn Sigler.

In 2006, she conceptualized and oversaw the first annual ***Giving Back 30***, a list of the largest public donations made by celebrities to charity. The list was released in *People* magazine and picked up in media around the world. In 2005, Stephanie conceptualized and produced the first annual ***12 Reasons to Give*** celebrity philanthropy calendar honoring 12 high-profile individuals who had donated at least one million dollars to charity. Athletes and entertainers honored in the inaugural calendar included Andre Agassi, Alonzo Mourning, David Robinson, Angelina Jolie, and Leonardo DiCaprio. Time Warner donated ad space for the project valued at more than $3 million. Through worldwide media coverage the calendar is estimated to have reached more than 110 million people.

The calendar and ***The Giving Back 30*** list were designed to highlight philanthropic role models and promote philanthropy. As a leader in celebrity philanthropy, Stephanie is often asked by the media to provide background and research for related articles. A strong proponent of philanthropic best practices and collaboration, Stephanie is leveraging The Giving Back Fund's 13 years of industry experience to develop programs that promote and celebrate "Best Practices" of successful athlete and celebrity philanthropy.

Stephanie brings to GBF 10 years of experience within the financial services industry at State Street Bank, Fidelity, and First Data Corporation. She holds a Bachelor of Fine Arts from Emerson College and is a published poet.

The Giving Back Fund's vision is, "A society in which becoming a successful philanthropist is as valued and desirable a goal as success in athletics, business, entertainment, or any other field."

As a national public charity, their goals are:

- To help cultivate a new group of philanthropists within the entertainment and sports industries, with a particular emphasis on groups often underrepresented in traditional philanthropy such as people of color, women, and youth.
- To help establish philanthropic role models who will inspire others to give back to their communities and create a high-profile, mutually supportive charitable community that works together in support of a diverse range of missions and goals.
- To honor philanthropy in all of its aspects, whether manifested by the giving of time, talent, or money to assist others.
- To encourage and support new philanthropy by offering professional, strategic, and cost-effective philanthropic consulting and management services.

Stephanie shared more about The Giving Back Fund:

> Marc Pollick established The Giving Back Fund in 1997 out of Boston. He got the inspiration after seeing how many sports-related foundations had troubles because oftentimes they were managed by people who did not have the experience. The intentions were really good, but they would end up getting in some trouble because they did not know how to remain in compliance with IRS requirements. We have grown from our original intent from how to distribute funds and program funding as over the years we realized a big component

of what we are doing is actually educating young athletes about philanthropy and the responsibilities of fame. We pretty much can do anything a client needs in philanthropy. We complement what they already have existing. So if somebody already has a 501c3, we will work with them under that 501c3 and if they have current employees or family members who want to get involved, we work with them as well. We are pretty much soup to nuts or we can fill in the blanks.

For example, the Yao Ming Foundation gets its tax-exempt status from The Giving Back Fund. There is no separate entity called the Yao Ming Foundation. It's really a component fund of The Giving Back Fund so our board is its board and we are legally responsible for everything that happens in its name. We work closely with Yao and his team of representatives to come up with our grant-making priorities, any programming, special events, etc.

The legal aspect of our work is so important, because many athletes aren't fully aware of all the tax obligations. We end up getting a lot of athletes come to us who have established 501c3s who are in trouble around those nonprofits. They may not have done the filing they were supposed to do; they may owe some kind of penalty. We work to make sure the penalties are reduced as much as possible. I think there is a misconception that exists of what is required to have a foundation. Many athletes establish foundations without understanding all the work that goes into it. If they did understand that they might choose to partner with existing charities or do something a little different than start their own.

We really try to encourage athletes to partner with existing charities to learn more about philanthropy before they establish an independent foundation. We set up donor advisory funds that an athlete will call a foundation. Then a year or two will go by and they will say, "You know, I really don't want all this responsibility," so we'll work with them to find a good charity that matches their values.

We have criteria for our client selection and are getting even stricter. We are changing our model from where we started. When you begin a company it's hard to be selective but we have been around for a while and are now developing some guidelines that we need to have the board pass in terms of the personal commitment that clients are willing to make. These requirements are not just financial, but include a willingness to be in touch with us. We're often asked if we are just dealing with handlers and we say no. We have found over the years that if you are not directly and regularly in touch with the athlete, it just doesn't work. You never know what they are hearing and what people are advising them so we make regular contact mandatory. There are still a few grandfather cases that we took on years and years ago where we don't have regular contact with the athlete and we are slowly starting to shut those down. Moving forward, if an athlete is not available to communicate with us then we will not be working with him or her. Holding athletes accountable for their charitable work is often a deterrent, and we currently turn away more business than we accept.

Another factor that plays an important role in the success or failure of a foundation is the athlete's personality. That can be partly because somebody is more personable than another and can really connect with the community. I think again that there has been a history within sports and entertainment with people establishing foundations because they have seen their peers do it. They might think it's just having a special event. Because they are celebrities, they think the money is just going to fly in, but it's actually a very competitive market—even with celebrities. So if you have a very special event, getting sponsorship still is a challenge. It's still a lot of work. I think what happens sometimes is that the athlete will get involved thinking it's a lot easier in part because their lifestyles train them that they get stuff for free and things just sort of happen for them. But it's really the first introduction to business for a lot of the athletes and it's a shock. When they get started their intentions are almost always good. When you sit down with the athletes they really care, but they don't necessarily know how to translate that caring into having an impact.

In order to have a successful philanthropic foundation, young athletes should first partner with a charity and see how they like that because it's less responsibility than having your own. If you can't handle that, you will see what's required. If you are going to have your own foundation and raise money, aside from your own money, you're going to have to make phone calls, you're going to have to show up places, you're going to have to be on time. All these negative stories that are almost cliché for our athletes and celebrities are based in some truth. If you're somebody who can't commit to being somewhere three months in advance then you should not have your own foundation.

I fear that more athletes will fall back into the old pattern of hiring the brother, sister, or father to run their foundations, and they won't be run like the businesses they are. There are a lot of rules and regulations that you need to keep in mind—best practices—and when you're working with professional athletes or celebrities, there are people who want to take advantage of them. You have to almost have an instinct of who those people are. I have been doing this for a long time and have developed a sense for it. Often a family can get blinded by previous friendships with these people and don't realize that they're being taken advantage of.

In the future, The Giving Back Fund will probably be working with fewer professional athletes on larger scale projects. We are also looking into mixing up our clients so that they are not all high-profile people.

Stephanie Sadler's Points to Ponder

- We try to encourage athletes to partner with existing charities to learn more about philanthropy before they establish an independent foundation.
- When you sit down with athletes, they really care, but they don't necessarily know how to translate that caring into having an impact.
- If you're somebody who can't commit to being somewhere three months in advance then you should not have your own foundation.

Steve Smith: The Veteran

Not only do I admire Steve Smith's charitable work, I have been a fan ever since he went to the NBA. As a child growing up, I lived across from a great person and ballplayer named Lorenzo "Lo" Neely. When you grow up with people, sometimes you don't have an appreciation of them like the rest of the world. Lo was standout player at Detroit Northern High School and part of the Eastern Michigan University 1991 Sweet 16 Team. He was and still is a great guy, role model, and friend. In 1989, I was across the street with his little brother and my friend Mo (I know, Lo and Mo) and there were some other guests at the home. It was future first-round pick Derrick "DC" Coleman and another young man sitting in the shadows. Because of Derrick's dominance at Syracuse, I was totally focused on him, even as Mo tugged my shirt and murmured in his low voice that Steve Smith from Michigan State University was sitting right there. I didn't care; I was all into DC. I even touched the oil that may have dripped from his car just to say, "I touched DC's car oil," even though I don't think his car was leaking. At any rate, little did I know I was not only amongst one superstar in DC, who has been committed to the revitalization of Detroit; I was amongst a future NBA and Philanthropy Champion, Steven Delano Smith.

Now retired from the NBA and an analyst on NBA TV, Steve is an avid golfer. I partly have him to blame for my addiction to the sport. When I was with Governor Granholm's staff I visited with him at his annual charity golf outing, which took place at the pristine Walnut Hills in Okemos, Michigan. Although I was just starting with golf and had yet to play a full 18 holes, I always traveled with my clubs and a change of clothes in the car. After talking with Steve about ways the governor could assist his philanthropic efforts, he invited me to play in his group during the outing. What followed was probably me giving one of the worst performances at a golf outing. However, my passion had begun and still exists to this day. The bad part was after playing with him at a beautiful country club, playing my next round at an economically challenged public course was quite a disappointment. At any rate, what follows is more information about the Steve Smith Charitable Foundation.

The Steve Smith Charitable Fund was established by former NBA and Michigan State University basketball star Steve Smith to honor those who helped support him in achieving his goals: his family, friends, teachers, coaches, and community. These people continue to inspire Steve and compel him to give back to the community.

The Steve Smith Pershing High MSU Scholarship for Academic Achievement benefits worthy and capable students enrolled at Michigan State University from Steve's hometown high school, Detroit Pershing High. The charity has since grown to meet broader needs in the communities that have supported Steve throughout his life.

The scholarship is a gift for the students so they may attend MSU without the burden of financing their education. This endowed scholarship is also intended to encourage students who have demonstrated the capacity to achieve educational and professional goals, the motivation to reach these goals, and the initiative to seek opportunities that will further their progress. Currently, the scholarship provides for $10,000 per student per academic year.

In the future, the Steve Smith Charitable Fund would like to bring even more students from Pershing High School to Michigan State University, and be able to provide funding for increasing tuition and room and board expenses, summer classes, and study abroad programs. It wants to act as a resource through which students may be able to find jobs and internships related to their field of study. For more information, please visit: www.stevesmithcharitablefund.org.

JASON RICHARDSON—THE STATESMAN

I had the pleasure of working with another Michigan State Spartan, Jason Richardson, and his Jason Richardson Foundation. I first met Jason at a Russell Simmons' "Get Your Money Right" conference. Panelists included Russell Simmons, Eminem, Common, Master P, and Suze Orman. When I talked to Jason, I was extremely impressed with how down-to-earth he was, considering he was an NBA Star and Slam Dunk Champion. He gave me some unique insight when I asked why so few NBA and professional athletes publicly give back. His answer was that so many players have been "burned" by schemes that they are reluctant and hesitant to get involved with new people or projects. That stuck with me. It was not until several years later, while in my role as a Government Relations and Public Affairs manager for Walmart, that I was able to assist Jason and his foundation.

During the 2010 NBA All-Star Game Weekend in Los Angeles, the Jason Richardson Foundation hosted its Man-Up Forum. I was proud to present the JRF with a check from Walmart for $50,000 to continue to support their great efforts.

The Jason Richardson Foundation was created to promote initiatives important to Jason, both locally and on a national spectrum. The foundation provides scholarship assistance, training and development opportunities, and builds greater awareness for issues and programs that Jason advocates. He aims to make a lasting impact in the lives of youth around the globe. The Foundation's Mission Statement is, "...committed to effectuating change in the lives of youth around the world. We are focused on making an impact on social issues that affect today's youth such as fatherlessness, disparities in education, and negative self-images that plague the minds of our youth. We will work tirelessly to protect the world's greatest commodity, its youth."

The Foundation's programs include:

THE MAN-UP FORUM

This is an open forum to all men of the community that encourages dialogue among boys and men. In this forum boys and men are challenged to bridge the communication gap between fathers and sons. The boys are encouraged to ask questions and share their experiences on a plethora of issues that directly impact their lives. This forum encourages the men to "Man Up" to their responsibilities and take accountability for their actions and reflect how their actions affect their families, most importantly their sons. All areas of life are discussed bar none.

Talk To The B.R.I.M. (Bold, Responsible, Intelligent, Mature)

A mentoring program designed for young women ages 10 thru 19. This program has been designed to manage the concerns of young women, their self-esteem, and negative self-images. There is a core component that places emphasis on "Single Parent Moms" and overcoming the obstacles that most often affect them.

The major function of TTB is to effectuate change in the lives of young women. (Girl chat, to empower and inspire!) Its goal is to remove rough exteriors through training and mentoring to reveal the beautiful diamond that lies beneath the surface. The core belief is that every young woman has value and our mission is to help each of them realize their potential.

Jason definitely has more to give and will continue to have a national impact with his unique and innovative programming. To learn more about Jason's foundation go to: www.jasonrichardsonfoundation.org.

Jalen Rose— "Mr. Swagger"

Probably most known for being the pivotal, vocal leader of America's bad boys of college basketball, the University of Michigan's "Fab Five," Jalen Rose seems to always be in the spotlight. He ushered in the new era of dress for college basketball and pop culture with the Fab Five's black socks and long baggy shorts. Now his primary role is as an NBA Analyst on ESPN, but more importantly, Jalen deserves acclaim for being a leader and teacher as he welcomes the inaugural class of the Jalen Rose Leadership Academy in Detroit.

A philanthropist who truly gives from the heart, Jalen established the Jalen Rose Foundation to create life-changing opportunities for underserved youth through the development of unique programs and the distribution of grants to qualified nonprofit organizations. The grants focus on education and sports and are distributed in Jalen's hometown of Detroit as well as other communities in need. More than $1.2 million in charitable donations have been distributed since the foundation's 2000 inception. Most recently, Jalen won the Community Champion Award from Black Enterprise for his outreach efforts in Detroit and was nominated for the prestigious Jefferson Award.

Jalen Rose spoke with me about what philanthropy means to him.

> Philanthropy is not always about money. It's about time, energy, resources, and caring about somebody who is not as fortunate and is in need at the time. When I became an NBA player, it gave me the resources to

give back to those who were less fortunate because I knew what it was like to be in those same positions.

Philanthropy comes from the heart and a lot has to do with your upbringing—staying grounded, staying humble, and not being willing to forget about those in the plight you left behind. It's a cycle that when you get the opportunity to live in the best neighborhoods, we move to the suburbs, we get an opportunity to shop at the best malls, we buy the Italian designers, it's just the cycle that is set up in America. So based on that, I always knew that there were those who were left behind and I was always doing what I could to uplift them as much as possible.

When I speak to youngsters about getting an education—children, high school, college students, and beyond—I stress that getting a degree, the Reading, Writing and Arithmetic—is only a part of that. People underestimate that the primary role of an education is to allow you to reason and make quality choices and decisions. At least it puts you in a position to not only be educated and smart, but it gives you an opportunity to understand what's right and what's wrong and how you use those platforms. Some student-athletes are the first to go to college from their family and probably the first to go to college in the neighborhood. They understand this motto I often use: The eight most important years of a student-athlete's life are the four years in high school and the four years that they are supposed to be in college. Because if you ask any adult whom did not achieve what they wanted to achieve in life and made poor choices and poor career decisions, often they point back to that eight-year window when things started to go off course.

This doesn't only apply to the students who play professionally. No matter what your goal, you need to be a student of your craft. If you say you want to be something, I'm all about it. Don't tell me you want to be in the NBA and I ask you how many teams are in the NBA and you don't know. As a student-athlete, if your goal and your dream is to go to the NBA, you should be just as passionate about other areas of your life. Have other interests. If the NBA is your goal, there are thousands of careers that come with being an athlete that have nothing to do with wearing a uniform. There are marketers, promoters, advertisers, doctors, lawyers, agents, and managers. The list goes on and on. There is a plethora of career opportunities.

It's so important that students are aware of other opportunities available in sports and entertainment. Even if you're fortunate enough to achieve your ultimate goal or dream in sports or entertainment, there is still a large portion of the day left remaining. You can only play football for three or four hours a day. You still have 20 more hours every day to be an industry, to be a brand, to be a productive member of society. People have been very receptive to that idea, but it's unfortunate that all too often we are just exposed to what we see on TV. We see the person in front of the camera in the uniform but need to pay attention to the fact that the people behind the camera are the ones in the administrative office; they are the ones in power.

We need to recognize the importance of education. Gone are the days where students can drop out of high school, or graduate from high school and go into the auto industry and make more money than their parents. Those days are gone. These students are dealing with a global economy and technology. They want to put their resume on a desk with kids from China, Japan, and the Philippines, where students are going to school six, seven days a week and learn multiple languages and have a tremendous amount of skills. So now the competition is fiercer and the job opportunities are that much smaller. It's very important to be multi-versed in whatever you want to get accomplished in your life.

I try to show these kids that you have to think long term in life. Don't think short term. You can't have the drug-dealer, street mentality that I'm only going to be here for a short window. What gives you longevity besides being healthy and taking care of yourself and making responsible decisions is being educated, being around quality people, being in the right place at the right time. Having multiple things that you're passionate about that you spend your time doing that put you in a position to have a career. I didn't just wake up yesterday and start working in the media; Mass Communications was my major at Michigan. I was in the media while I was playing. I have been retired five years; I have been working in the media for 10 years. I got traded from the Pacers, where for the six and a half years I was there we had the top record in the NBA, to the Bulls, where we had nine wins by February. So I said I guess I'm not going to be in the playoffs this year. So I started getting media gigs. I started working for *The Best Damn Sports Show*, I did sideline for TNT, and I did halftime with ABC. I just stayed on my grind.

That type of long-term planning, that longevity, has allowed mainstream America to appreciate who I am as a person beyond basketball. It's only about survival.

The next generation of student and professional athletes has to work faster. When we were in college growing up, we had to go back to the dorm room to check the voicemail to see where the party was that night or to see if our girlfriends called us or not. Now students just look down at the beeper to see who's beeping with the code. They have to be sharper; they have to be faster. My five-year-old daughter has an iPad. She can work it; she can get online; she can do everything she has to do. These young brothers have to be sharper, bigger, stronger, faster, more disciplined. There's more stuff coming at them than before. There's cursing on the radio now. I remember hiding my tapes that had curse words on them so my mother wouldn't even think I was listening to my Too Short or N.W.A.

We came up in the Oven Generation. We had to allow things to simmer. We appreciated the nine to five; we appreciated the neighbor down the street who worked 40 hours a week and then he wanted to get his extra hours so he worked double time. We appreciated the A-Plan. We appreciated having to shovel snow, cut grass, pump gas, and work as paperboys. We had to do those things not only to have something for ourselves but also to have some self-esteem and responsibility. Now that's lost. They're the Microwave Generation. The instant-message generation. They can't have a conversation without using bad abbreviations. A lot of them are parents of crack babies, irresponsible parents. Knowing that they didn't have success in their life, they're still sitting in the living room letting a seven-year-old watch *Scarface*.

I wanted to get into education because I felt like I was old enough to still be cool. I know who Lil Wayne is; I know who Young Jeezy is; I have a Twitter account; I have a Facebook page. I know what the style is, yet I'm old enough to be retired and have some knowledge about what it takes to be a college student, a college athlete, what it takes to be a leader in the community, what it takes to work for a conglomerate and a big company like Disney/ESPN and ABC. I'm trying to uplift as many people as I can.

I hope kids look at me and think they can still be cool and be corporate. And sometimes we go overboard. Instead of having on big shorts we wear our pants hanging off our ass showing our groin. Instead of having one or two tattoos we have to have tattoos on our neck. We go overboard. Beyond that, what young adults need to understand, especially if they're black is, before you open your mouth, people are going to judge 80% of what they think about you by your appearance. You don't even have to open your mouth.

At our academy, there are 120 students per grade, 480 students total. It's heart-wrenching because they're chosen by a lottery. But at the end of the day you have to tell yourself, I'm trying to help as many people as possible so if I'm touching one person in a positive manner that's what my goal and my job is. It so happens that I'm fortunate to do 120 times four.

First and foremost we want a safe learning environment. We will have kids coming in and out of there from 8:30 a.m. to 4:30 p.m. We need to make sure that they're safe in there and that everyone in the neighborhood is responsible. That's the most important thing. That's why Country Day, Catholic Central, or University of Liggett are not in Detroit. It's very important to have a safe learning environment.

The next thing is that I want JRLA to be community orientated and community friendly. My job is not only to have a great public school. We have been trained to think that Cass Tech and Renaissance are Country Day and they are not. You ask any Detroiter what the best school in Detroit is and they say Cass Tech and Renaissance. There has never been a third; there has never been a fourth. There has never been anything else. At JRLA, I'm trying to create a University of Liggett in the city.

I really appreciate what you're doing with your book. The most refreshing thing about all this is that we have the same goal. We are trying to uplift our city. That's our goal. What's crucial about your project is you're giving them something that they actually have to read. Sometimes with the Internet, tweeting, iPad and iPhone, kids don't even read books. Not only are you giving them something that's for them, but also hopefully it's giving them the passion to want to read.

I think there will be comparisons with Andre Agassi's charter school in Las Vegas. I was actually disappointed when I got into philanthropy and realized that the only athletes and entertainers who have charter schools are Andre Agassi, Kevin Johnson, George Gerving, David Robinson, and Oprah Winfrey. David Robinson's is a private school. There are so many influential people who can pick up a phone and snap a finger and raise the $10 million I'm trying to raise. So that disappointed me getting into this but it motivated me also. So if we are compared to what Andre Agassi is doing, that's terrific because he's doing a great thing.

My obligations with ESPN have me working 10-15 days a month. That's from late October when NBA season starts until June. So when we have opening day for school, I'm going to be there. When it's time for summer school and summer programs and getting to know the families, I'm going to be there. I'm trying to meet every family. I'm going to sit down and talk to every kid before they come to school.

To learn more about Jalen's foundation, visit www.jalen-rose.com/the-jalen-rose-charitable-fund.

Jalen Rose's Points to Ponder

- Philanthropy is not always about money. It's about time, energy, resources, and caring about somebody who is not as fortunate and is in need at the time.
- As a student-athlete, if your goal and your dream is to become a student-athlete, you should be just as passionate about other areas of your life. Have other interests.
- I hope kids look at me and think they can still be cool and corporate.

Conclusion

"Life is an echo—what you send out comes back."
—Unknown

In the United States, wealth is highly concentrated in relatively few hands. As of 2007, the top 1% of households (the upper class) owned 34.6% of all privately held wealth, and the next 19% (the managerial, professional, and small business stratum) had 50.5%, which means that just 20% of the people owned a remarkable 85%, leaving only 15% of the wealth for the bottom 80% (wage and salary workers). In terms of financial wealth (total net worth minus the value of one's home), the top 1% of households had an even greater share: 42.7%. This is drawn from the careful work of economist Edward N. Wolff at New York University (2010).

It's argued the wealth creates jobs, business opportunities, and philanthropy. However, that is a theory that does not seem to have been most impactful on society.

Trickle Down Theory?

A free society allows for certain talent to be the driving engine for ambition and success. This eventually allows individuals to help others—if they choose. Wealth and inequality is possibly at an all-time high in the United States. This concentration of wealth is focused on a small percentage of the population, which includes professional athletes.

Statistically, high net worth charitable giving accounts for about two-thirds of all individual giving and about one-half of all charitable giving in the United States. Unfortunately, according to the "2010 Study of High Net Worth Philanthropy" by Bank of America/Merrill Lynch (a biennial study done in partnership with the Center on Philanthropy at Indiana University), charities have to make do with less. Median charitable giving by high net worth households dropped 7.6% from 2007 to 2009. Average charitable giving fared even worse, declining an astonishing 34.9% from 2007 to 2009. The cause for these declines is the "Great Recession," which began in December 2007 and supposedly ended in June 2009.

The 2010 study follows the same methodology as the 2006 and 2008 studies. It reflects the responses of more than 800 households randomly surveyed in affluent neighborhoods across the United States. Households in the study have an income of greater than $200,000 and/or a net worth of at least $1 million, excluding the value of their primary residence. The average wealth of the respondents was more than $10 million, and half of all respondents had a net worth of between $3 million and $20 million. Access to the full 75-page 2010 study is available at http://www.philanthropy.iupui.edu/Research/docs/2010BAML_HighNetWorthPhilanthropy.pdf

This is all the more reason why a movement of student-athletes and student-leaders donating their time to charity will have significant impact, because there is a great need. Philanthropy provides student-athletes and student-leaders an opportunity to interact with positive role models and get involved in community service projects. It encourages personal growth and development, thus having an overall positive impact on society as a whole.

Volunteering

Volunteering remains a significant part of the philanthropic efforts of wealthy individuals. Since 2007, high net worth households have been increasing the amount of time they give to organizations and causes they value. Nearly 79% of high net worth individuals volunteered in 2009, and the percentage who volunteered more than 200 hours a year rose significantly, from 27% in 2007 to 39% in 2009. The study also found, not surprisingly, that the more high net worth individuals volunteered, the more they gave. For example, non-volunteers donated $46,414 on average in 2009, while those who volunteered more than 200 hours donated $75,662 to charity last year. The rise in volunteerism, according to the study, may be due to a combination of factors, including a tendency among donors to compensate for financial constraints during a time of recession by committing more of their time, skills, and other human capital. Another factor may be that baby boomers have begun to retire or scale back on their working hours, leaving more time for volunteer efforts.

The key point from this study of the charitable efforts of wealthy individuals is that the more high net worth individuals volunteered, the more they gave. How often do athletes and others say, "When I get my money right, I will start a foundation"? This study supports the idea that the sooner student-athletes get involved in charitable giving, the more likely they will increase their giving as their net worth increases. So starting them early can make them huge philanthropists throughout their lifetimes.

This work will take a steady effort. That's why coaches are so important. In many cases they have more access and influence to the student-athletes than their parents or other family members. Often coaches are the only ones who can hand out penalties and punishments that will be adhered to. A slow and steady influence will make a lasting impact.

Philanthropy can be universally described as giving. Attributes of giving are love and compassion. It's almost like you are tricking the student-athletes into promoting love and compassion amongst their family, friends, and community. Greater promotion of love and compassion will be some of the several by-products of exposing student-athletes to philanthropy.

There is one team you can never get cut from, one position that you can't be replaced at, injury will not stop you from competing and everyone can become a champion, and that is the game of Philanthropy!

PROFESSIONAL DEVELOPMENT AND FINANCIAL LITERACY

During Chapter 2, I discussed how I realized that in order for the next generation to become philanthropic, they had to become employed and properly manage the money they earn before they can give it away. Here are 10 Steps for Professional Development and Financial Literacy. These lists are not exhaustive, but offer some examples that can help you along the way.

10 STEPS TO HELP YOU IN YOUR PROFESSIONAL DEVELOPMENT

- Take care in your appearance—How you look is how you will be addressed
- Ask questions—Show interest in the position and bring extra copies of your resume
- Be confident—It is okay to sell yourself and speak highly about your skill set
- Show a positive attitude—Your attitude determines your altitude
- Learn to take constructive criticism
- Be prompt—On time is late (be 15 minutes early)
- Display integrity—All you have in this world is your word...your word is all you have

- Research the company and the job—Knowing is half the battle
- Remember it's just business; it's not personal—Remain professional and don't let friendships get in the way of business
- Be mindful of the 10-foot rule—Always speak and acknowledge a person when within 10 feet of him or her

Financial Literacy

- Don't assume credit cards will save you.
- Resist impulse buying
- Have a saving goal
- Pay yourself first by saving first
- Don't allow your savings to be easily accessible
- Know the difference between something you need and something you want
- Don't take out college loans (or any other loan) if you really don't have to
- Learn about interest rates; they make the item cost more and you must pay it back
- Be careful with your personal information to prevent identity theft

PHILANTHROPY AND THE 10 STEPS TO BECOMING A PHILANTHROPIST

Philanthropy—"the love of humanity"—love in the sense of caring for, nourishing, developing, or enhancing—humanity. In modern practical terms, it is "private initiatives for public good, focusing on quality of life."

Learning is done by example; if one never sees or experiences philanthropy at a young age, s/he is less likely to give as an adult. There will also be another generation that is not exposed to philanthropy and the cycle of non-giving will continue.

Philanthropy is a difficult concept to accept, especially for those coming from a background of little to no means. "How can I talk about giving to someone else when I don't have anything?" That is a very real statement, especially when you take into account the many economic challenges facing the nation. Also, one can alienate others and sound like an elitist based on how and to whom they present the philanthropic discussion. However, what younger generations need to know is that being philanthropic is not only about giving money. That is a key part of philanthropy when you talk about fundraisers and capital campaigns. However philanthropy also includes giving something as valuable as money—your time. One could argue that your time is more valuable than money because money comes and goes but you can't get time back. So even if one is not in a position to give financially, almost anyone can give his or her time. Once a person begins to give his or her time to be philanthropic, giving money will come much easier. So we need to start with the promotion of "giving what you can, even if it's just your time."

10 Steps to Becoming a Philanthropist

Among the many other definitions for philanthropy is the practice of performing charitable or benevolent actions. While many philanthropists are well off, the true definition of the word refers to performing charitable acts, not necessarily spending money. So with that, let's start you on your way to becoming a philanthropist.

1. Pick an issue that is to close to you. An example could be cancer research, education reform, or providing fresh drinking water.
2. Educate yourself on that issue. One Internet search can bring a world of information to your computer screen. Also, social media platforms like Facebook, Twitter, and World Press are excellent tools to learn more about a particular issue.
3. Find family and friends who may support that same cause.
4. Find local groups and organizations that may support that same cause as well. Churches and institutions of higher learning (community colleges and universities) normally have local organizations that are involved in every issue imaginable.
5. Volunteer!! Roll up your sleeves and dive right in. If you're passionate about this issue, it will be more fun than work.
6. Report back to your network what you have experienced.

7. Recruit, because every great cause needs help.
8. Make your own project. Now that you have learned more about the issue, found a network of support, and recruited others to get involved, you can find your own project to work on. You will be able to bring a unique perspective to addressing and solving this problem.
9. Debrief. After you have completed your project, debrief about it. Share your findings with others so your work can be critiqued to be most effective and your findings can be passed on to others so not to have done the project in vain.
10. Repeat for effect!! That's right, do it again and again so to have the most impact on the cause you are working toward.

Now you're a philanthropist, one who performs charitable and benevolent actions. Thank you so much, the world needed that.